Roles

CHOICES

GUIDES FOR TODAY'S WOMAN

Roles

Brunetta R. Wolfman

The Westminster Press
Philadelphia

Book Design by Alice Derr

First edition

Published by The Westminster Press®
Philadelphia, Pennsylvania

PRINTED IN THE UNITED STATES OF AMERICA

9   8   7   6   5   4   3   2   1

Library of Congress Cataloging in Publication Data

Wolfman, Brunetta R., 1931–
  Roles.

  (Choices : guides for today's woman)
  1. Women—United States—Social conditions.
  2. Women—United States—Psychology. 3. Sex role—
  United States. 4. Social role. 5. Role conflict.
  6. Afro-American women. I. Title. II. Series.
  HQ1426.W57 1983   305.4′2′0973   83-12441
  ISBN 0-664-24542-0 (pbk.)

CONTENTS

68257

PUBLISHER'S ACKNOWLEDGMENT

The publisher gratefully acknowledges the advice of several distinguished scholars in planning this series. Virginia Mollenkott, Arlene Swidler, Phyllis Trible, and Ann Ulanov helped shape the goals of the series, identify vital topics, and locate knowledgeable authors. Views expressed in the books, of course, are those of the individual writers and not of the advisers.

CHAPTER 1

Introduction: What Are Women Supposed to Be Doing?

> All the world's a stage,
> And all the men and women merely players:
> They have their exits and their entrances;
> And one man in his time plays many parts.
> —Shakespeare, *As You Like It*

Who are you? What parts do you play? When we are born, we are daughter, perhaps sister, and often granddaughter. As we grow older, we add new roles to the original ones; we become playmate, student, neighbor, wife, mother, and even grandmother. None of us are so one-dimensional that we have only one role. It is impossible to be a fully functioning human being without having many roles. The word "role" is derived from the theatrical term and is part of the glue that holds societies together. Roles are the parts we play in any situation and the ways in which we behave that fit those situations.

There are some roles we have from birth and never think about because they are a part of our lives. We may ponder the implications and meaning of being a daughter, cousin, sweetheart, wife, mother, sister, aunt; but we seldom have to think about how to behave in those roles. That is because there are simple patterns of behavior and expectations that guide our actions and responses when we assume those roles. Even though relationships may become complicated on the most basic level, we all tend to know what a daughter is expected to do or be.

Why are we as women particularly concerned with our roles in today's world? Partly because we and those around us have changing ideas about what we should be doing. As we move from childhood to adulthood we acquire new roles and modify previous ones. Much of this learning process is made fairly easy by established cultural patterns. Formerly, even as adults women played roles primarily within the family, but now a great many women are assuming roles in the world of work for pay.

Although some jobs have long been open to women, others have not. The titles teacher, social worker, and secretary conjure up images of women, and most people are comfortable with these images. When doctor, minister, or engineer is mentioned, images of men may come to mind. Women may experience feelings of ambiguity when they assume a role that has traditionally been a male one. They may experience difficulty and even encounter hostility from others when their roles do not correspond to popular images.

Yet many women handle a wide range of roles, including nontraditional ones, with unconscious ease. This was shown vividly to me once when I led a workshop session for women working in higher education. I asked each member of the group to introduce herself and tell the others some of the roles she played on a daily basis. Generally when women are asked to list their roles, they begin with those describing an association with relatives or friends. Then they go on to the roles describing skills, status at work or in the community, or personal characteristics. These particular women mentioned many aspects of their lives: jobs, relationships, personal styles, duties, hobbies, organizations belonged to, age, and others. Here are the titles that these twenty women used to describe themselves: administrator, advocate, arbitrator, committee member, conciliator, church member, catalyst, clerk, curriculum developer, faculty wife, graduate student's wife, job developer, family banker, gardener, home decorator, hedonist, mediator, organizer, politician, second wife, talent groomer, adviser, athlete, community activist, daughter, mentor, fighter, housekeeper, learner, planner, recruiter, single parent, trainer, breadwinner, coordinator, volunteer, divorced woman, friend, idealist, lone woman in the office, mother, policy implementer, researcher, single woman, wife, analyst, lover, mother-in-law, colleague, counselor, faculty member, graduate student, implementer, manager, older woman, risk taker, supervisor, young woman. The list amazed us and made us realize how complex our lives were. One woman said, "I get tired just hearing all the things that we do."

Some of our roles we inherit, some we grow into, and others come with our jobs. Most of our ideas of behavior appropriate to roles are transmitted through traditions of our families, which communicate values of our ethnic group, religious tradition, and economic class. These expectations of roles and behavior are transmitted by what people say and do or through informal and formal teaching about the culture.

SOURCES OF ROLES

Our first encounters with family help us determine proper behavior and responsibilities as girls and women. We learn from our mothers or female guardians how we females should act and what limits are set for us. Can we run and jump, climb trees, cook, get dirty, yell, and "act out" in school? The first lessons are wordless; later come the stories from family lore.

Amy, Betsy, and Carol have different traditional expectations for a daughter and woman. In Amy's family, the women were home all day, taking care of children, cleaning, cooking, and visiting with women relatives and neighbors. The little girls were kept in sight of mama or the other female relatives and encouraged to imitate mother in doing her chores. When the family gathered, the men ate first, discussing politics or work. When they had finished eating, the women came in from the kitchen and, over food, continued conversations about family wants, children, or chores.

Betsy remembers that her mother was a teacher and loved to tell her family of the antics and frustrations of working with students from immigrant families. The stories about her mother's schoolteaching surprised Betsy because her mother was always home when Betsy came in from her own school. The family gathered for dinner when Betsy's father returned from his office. Although women prepared the food, they sat at table to discuss church and friends.

Carol's mother was often away from home, busy as a volunteer with church or YWCA or Girl Scout work. For help with housework she hired a weekly cleaning lady, and everything always seemed to be in order. She entertained her church and community groups with brunches, luncheons, and teas. When the family gathered on festive occasions, there was always a hired woman in the kitchen to serve the food which she and Carol's mother had prepared.

Amy, Betsy, and Carol all learned from experience that mothers were responsible for the house, meals, and general maintenance of the family. Most women have learned early on what is expected of them by observing their mothers or other female relatives. They also were taught how to act as daughters: to be respectful, polite, and attentive to womanly tasks.

Families often tell stories about their ancestors and tinge the telling with admiration or deprecation. Women who have had to assume nontraditional roles are described with approval or pity, thus communicating to youngsters what type of behavior is valued. Ethnically, the ways of the past and of the Old Country are often revealed as out of place in modern America. If each generation achieves beyond the generation before and the children are told that they will continue the pattern, the lesson is an important one for girls as well as for boys.

Religiously, too, women receive instruction about traditional roles. Some are told that women should be demure and deferential, as the Bible commands. Others are praised for their leadership in mixed groups.

POPULAR CULTURE

Next after the family as a source of roles is popular culture. We are always surrounded by popular culture: the music, movies, and literature of our society. We may learn from it unconsciously that girls are soft and full of moonbeams, made to be loved and cared for, waiting for the right man to come along. We read stories of romance in which the woman is rescued from all types of evil or danger. Although occasionally the heroine is a "girl detective" or a nurse, the traditional message is that a girl is weak and needs the protection of a male. Many women in the media are flighty and not too reliable, not physically strong, and perhaps scheming to make men think they are smart. The early television programs often showed women as happy housewives in the kitchen, baking cookies for the kids to devour when they came in from school. The mothers were typically scatterbrained though somewhat wise in the final scene. For many years the movies often showed a career girl who found happiness as wife to a man who would protect her from the problems of the work world. A determined woman who continued in a career was bound to be hard-bitten and bitter, rejecting the proper role of a woman and suffering the consequences. We all need to examine critically these kinds of lessons from popular culture. We must learn to choose what really fits us personally.

For example, Eveleyn's expectations of womanhood were based on magazine stories, movies, television, radio stories, and popular songs. She went through high school looking for the perfect type of makeup and clothes. She earnestly read advice about how to talk to boys and how to be popular. She was a cheerleader, sang in the church choir, went to socials, but felt miserable in trying to live up to images. She was pushed into college so that she would meet a better type of fellow to marry. She joined a sorority and did everything that was expected, but did not find a husband in college. She really did not mind except in being labeled "old maid" by her family and relatives. By the time she did meet a man she wanted to marry, she found that she had developed her own independent style. She had left behind the magazine and movie heroines; she was far from the stereotyped weak woman and certainly not the prim old maid. Her own unique qualities attracted her husband rather than those she had discarded.

REASONS FOR CONFLICT ABOUT ROLES

Since roles are defined by our families and cultural environment, we inherit many without realizing what they mean to us. Conflicts arise when the definitions of the role and our own feelings are dissimilar; this has been happening with increasing frequency in the past few years as women move into the masculine world of work. Over the past twenty years, more and more women have entered the labor force. Many reasons have promoted this change. Mostly, women went to work out of necessity. They were a part of an expanding labor force and an expanding economy; they were a part of the consumer revolution, craving to have the material goods advertised on television and in the press. Many women were also thrust into the labor force because of the economics of divorce. As increasing numbers of marriages failed, the wives became supporters of their families. If the father provided child support, it was often not enough to sustain a standard of living approximating the former standard. Other women sought employment because they had attained a level of education that encouraged them to work for independence and self-fulfillment. These women began to work to live up to the expectations of their families and of their professors. Some of the women in this group were fresh from college, while others had been housewives and mothers, returning to the labor force or entering it for the first time at a late age.

This last group provided the support and intellectual arguments for the women's movement as these women strove for promotions and satisfaction. Expecting that work would bring a sense of fulfillment, they considered low-level positions to be boring, unrewarding, and unrecognized. They found that women were seldom considered for promotion and risked being trapped in the same job until retirement. Ambitious women wanted to compete with men for good jobs. In order to do so, they began to observe and imitate the behavior of men in higher positions.

As women began working in greater numbers, the civil rights movement caused awareness of the need to extend opportunities to groups previously excluded. Articulate women analyzed the condition of women as being similar to that of minority groups and they urged change in discriminatory laws and behavior.

Such action against laws and discriminatory practices has had considerable success and has opened many doors to women. The numbers of women in influential positions in government, educational institutions, and businesses has increased. Women have been hired to work in many jobs formerly considered to be "male" jobs. We now see women in the police force, and as fire fighters, construction workers, and heads of businesses. In a sense, we have made many occupations sexless because they can be done by a person of either sex and are not reserved for only one group.

Change is almost never easy, and the changed expectations for women and their roles have resulted in many tensions and strains. These are played out in individual families and throughout our society. Change for women has been a prominent issue in the courts, legislatures, and political campaigns. The new status of women or the search for a new status operates on many levels. Many women are seeking a fair wage for a fair day's work. Others are seeking to develop their maximum potential and sense of self-fulfillment. There are other women who want to achieve the same as men have achieved, or more. They seek dominance over their environment and control of the world in which they work. They have helped give women's ambition a new respectability as they emulate men, attempting to succeed in the ways that men have used. They use as models the methods, the styles, and the dress of men in their attempts to win at the male game.

Tensions are caused not only by changing expectations but also varying definitions of women and their roles. These definitions of what a woman is and how she should behave range from the traditional to the radical.

There are those who believe in the subordination of women to men, following the literal interpretation of the biblical story in which Eve was told that Adam was to rule over her. This injunction along with other examples from the Bible is used to explain that women should be subservient to men and should submissively fulfill men's needs and expectations. In this view a woman is a "server" bound to traditional roles, living a life like her grandmother's. Such a woman's mission in life is to give birth to children and to nurture them and her husband. She may be cared for like a child and guided by a kindly father figure who is responsible for her welfare.

At the other end of the ideological spectrum are the radical feminists who maintain that women should be dominant. They define women in total isolation from men and see only difficulties between the sexes, a constant state of hostility. Such radicals either move away from involvement with men or they seek dominance. Such women may attribute the evils of the world to men's actions, but maintain that women's qualities are opposite and offer hope. Radicals may believe that women are oppressed victims dominated by male supremacists who control the political, cultural, and social institutions.

In between the extremes of submission and of radical defiance, most of us women keep trying to define ourselves and our roles. Should the behavior of women be based on definitions articulated by men? Or are there significant differences which need to be respected and understood? I want to help other women decide for themselves by examining some of the ways in which we function and handle our lives in ways unique to women.

There are many reasons for feeling hopeful about the chances of performing many roles well as a woman. Women learn new roles as they move from childhood to adolescence to womanhood. Typically we are able to handle multiple tasks and responsibilities with relative ease, as versatility is part of our essential character, a feminine quality. Complexity should be recognized as enhancing and not demoralizing. Women are able to do many things, if not all at once, then in a lifetime.

CHAPTER 2

Superwoman vs. Little Woman: Career Woman vs. Housewife

Stereotypes of women's roles complicate our understandings of ourselves. Whether we work primarily in the home or outside in paid employment, we encounter overly simple ideas of our life-styles. The reality is that each woman's life involves work, flexibility, and the need for compromises. Here we will first look carefully at contrasting general roles—housewife and career-oriented woman. We will find underlying similarities in the way these women cope with their roles.

WOMEN AT HOME AND IN THE WORKPLACE

HOUSEWIFE

Most women have learned that society expects them to be wives and mothers—and until recently middle-class values dictated that a woman be a housewife. This general role is defended by many older and traditionally-minded people, who maintain that being an effective wife and mother requires nearly all a woman's energies. From this standpoint, Vivian might be considered the ideal American wife and mother. Her husband is a manager in a financial company. The family lives in a lovely quiet suburban neighborhood where each of the three children has a room.

Flowers fill every nook and recess, adding to the air of dedicated graciousness. Vivian sums up her life quietly:

> "I'm trying to do the best that I can with the talents God gave me. I have a family, and I am trying to do the best that I can with them and for them by being a wife and mother and providing a home and love for those whom I care about. I feel that this is very important to my own well-being, not so much my feeling of self-fulfillment. I don't think that sense is so important for me. It is the way that I was brought up. What I feel is important to do with my life is to be independent and not be a slave, but to have the things which I consider to be most important, love and my family."

Though Vivian's home could provide a model of good taste in decorating, she is not a drudge. Her schedule includes cleaning and cooking, but it also allows time for her to serve on the boards of two community organizations, including a bank, be a member of the vestry of her church, and contribute time to the parents' group at the children's school. She manages to play tennis or to exercise regularly, and she plays the piano for her own relaxation. She plans activities for the family, and she and her husband regularly attend concerts or movies.

Vivian feels that she is happy and that her life is totally involving. However, some of her women peers treat her as if she is wasting her life and is not worth much because she is not working at a paid job. When she meets these women, they treat her as if she is a rare species, a spoiled, self-indulgent woman who is out of touch with the world. Others insinuate that she is a parasite or is lazy and wonder whether perhaps her children have special problems that she must cope with by staying home.

Vivian and her husband have talked about the possibility that she might go to work when the children are in college. She worked in an office before their first child was born. However, they agree that the way in which Vivian is conducting her life is best for them at their stage of life. The stresses are imposed from outside, but Vivian sidesteps them, saying:

> "You have to somehow decide that the negative things are not really that important. You move on positively and try to know people who are headed in the same direction as you."

CAREER WOMAN

When women go to work outside the home, if they have families, they are still expected to maintain the standards of full-time housewives. They must face comments such as: "Are you getting a divorce?" "Do your kids clean up by themselves?" "Her house must be dirty" and "You probably can't eat off her floors." Yet career-oriented women— single as well as married—must realistically have concern for domestic chores as well as for personal relationships.

Wilma is a confirmed career woman. "The time is short, but I make it count as much as I can." This might be one of the mottoes that has guided Wilma's life as she has risen steadily to the top of a large organization. She describes her schedule in the following manner:

> "I literally work eighteen hours a day, and sometimes maybe twenty. That's not five days a week; that's seven. Even with that kind of demanding schedule, and the sheer number of problems which come to me, I enjoy it. I enjoy work, diversity, different kinds of situations. I think that I am very conscientious about getting as much background information as possible. Obviously the more tasks one has to do, the more difficult it becomes, so it's always a matter of picking and choosing and learning which choices to rely on and how to get maximal information in the shortest period of time."

Wilma goes on to tell about herself and the type of person she is.

"I think that I am as I have always been. My basic pattern has always been the same. Many people describe me as an intense person, and for a while that bothered me. I felt that there was something wrong with being intense, but I'm not apologetic about it now. I was an intense student, even in grade school. I think that many people, most people, simply don't understand the degree of pressure, stress on a person in leadership. I realize that I am different. At first, it bothered me a little bit, but now I accept it. I don't think about it very much, and I don't resent the fact that other people don't understand my life. That's one of the prices, one of the consequences one accepts as part of this kind of position.

"I have less and less time for myself away from the job this year, and this situation concerns me. I have assumed more job-related activities and as a result I have not even been able to fly a plane for four or five months, something I find relaxing. There's almost never any time for me, and that's a problem. Concerning my children, my two boys, one is away at college. The other one lives with me. It has been a difficult year for him, because I work so much. If I am not out of town, I come home every evening between five thirty and six, and we chat as we often do when I get home at the end of the evening."

While the priorities are clearly different, Vivian, the housewife, and Wilma, the career woman, share basic concerns. Both are versatile women, playing a variety of different roles. Both spend time and effort at work, albeit differently defined. Both are careful to maintain relationships—with considerable loving investment in people. Both women combine public and private spheres. Wilma has sacrificed some professional opportunities to spend time with her son, and Vivian takes time from her family for community activities. Like most women they do not conform in every way to the stereotypes. Finally, both have

come to terms with stereotypes and feel content with their
own choice of a cluster of roles.

WOMEN AND WORK

Wilma's career offers much besides financial reward. It
offers a sense of helping others and of personal fulfillment.
She says:

> "I am really committed to what my profession can do
> for people, and it may be the only field I know of
> where you can effect the most change, for my children,
> their children, generations ahead. The other part of it
> is that I plainly like complexity. I like risks and
> diversity. I'm curious, and the job provides a marvel-
> ous opportunity to learn. You can explore lots of
> different problems and personalities. You can never
> be bored."

Wilma is fortunate because she loves what she is doing and
has committed herself, heart and soul, to her profession.
This may be one of the factors that has contributed to her
success, so that she finds herself leading her organization.
Unfortunately, most women who are employed are not in
positions that are exciting. The jobs are not a part of a career
ladder, nor could they be described in the altruistic terms of
Wilma's job. Most women set out to find jobs to supplement
their husband's paycheck or to provide the sole support of
their families. They are not destined to move up the
executive ladder. Advice on how to maneuver into the
executive suite is lost on them, because they will never
have an opportunity to achieve a supervisory or managerial
position. They are working for survival and have little zest
for a major job, nor are they likely to be considered for such
a position.

There is nothing wrong with having a job rather than a
career. A career usually requires educational preparation
and more of an emotional investment than a job requiring
no special qualifications. Many women who work outside
the home are conscientious and give their best effort on the

job. They may not have an emotional investment in the company, agency, or institution, but they have an investment in their own work and the standards which they set for that work.

Women approach their obligations in a similar manner whether they work inside or outside the home. In fact, there are many similarities in the way women work in the home and for wages. Many of the jobs filled by women are in service industries rather than in manufacturing, and provide service to customers rather than goods. Women are employed in the offices of the large service businesses, banks, insurance, and behind the counters of retail merchandising companies. They are considered support staff for those in the decision-making positions. Many of the aspects of their jobs are repetitious and routine, much like housework. The tasks are easily taught, and again, like homemaking, the quality of the work is not easily evident though the woman doing the work is aware of the quality of the effort. These support-staff positions, like housework, are not highly valued by those people who set the norms for our society.

There appears to have developed a false dichotomy between work inside and work outside the home. Perhaps it is because what men do on the job and at home is at variance, but historically women have had duties of a nature similar to their home roles. They have extended their nurturing into professional fields such as teaching, social work, nursing, and the traditional female clerical jobs. Even if women are now in nontraditional occupations, they do not and are not able to shut themselves off from the traditional home responsibilities. And this is one of the complaints that many working women have: they must combine housework and housewifery with full-time employment. One of the major differences is that the housewife controls her own time rather than having someone else determine how she will allocate her time to the necessary chores.

Though women complain about having to do housework while holding full-time jobs, most are able to combine the parts of their lives competently, but do so with stress. However, they do know how to handle multiple roles as a matter of course, as a natural part of their lives, because they have learned to do so as girls and only add to and change the nature of the roles as they mature.

Women may assume multiple roles and responsibilities, grumbling, but without undue strain because they have grown into being complex manipulators of roles as they grew into womanhood. One of the advantages of being an American female is that one learns how to handle more than one or two sets of tasks at the same time. There has been little discussion of this inherent ability, because there has been little examination of the ways in which women live their lives.

GIRLHOOD TRAINING FOR MULTIPLE ROLES

Since most of us wish to handle our many roles well, it is worthwhile to study other women who are both busy and effective. Although some scholars emphasize disadvantages for girls in doing fewer competitive sports than boys, it is clear that girls do learn valuable life skills—particularly the ability to adapt to a variety of roles.

Girls' training for multiple roles comes from a variety of sources: family examples and expectations, practice, school training, extracurricular activities, and values from important people.

FAMILY EXAMPLES AND EXPECTATIONS

Women who were asked when it was that they began to take on many responsibilities and activities found that as they dredged up memories, they could not ever remember doing "nothing." In fact, one woman described this situation:

"You know, it was funny, but everyone in my family simply had an expectation that people did things and people in the family would do things. There was no demand for a particular type of thing. There was just an unspoken understanding that everyone in the family would be involved with something."

Another woman, who is a single parent, remembers:

"I have no question about the fact that I was a super-responsible kid. I was super responsible to my parents, to my school, to my church. I was expected to be, and I thought it rather appropriate that I be responsible. I did it and not in the sense of fighting to make life easier. My own family was such that I not only felt responsible for myself but for my sister when she was growing up. I did well in school and loved it. I got lots of rewards for doing well. So it wasn't a bad deal."

The expectations were a part of the homelife of most women and they acted out those expectations as they grew from girlhood to adulthood. Anna, a busy woman, analyzed her early beginnings handling multiple roles:

"I was brought up in a Protestant home with the work ethic uppermost in our consciousness. I saw my father work twelve hours a day, and I was told that it was good to work hard, to like your work. I picked up that attitude and modified it for myself. I said to myself as I grew up that I would find work that I liked so that I would not be forced to like something that I just happened to stumble into. I did not want to find a job which was drudgery, because I would betray the work ethic in some way if I did that. I like to work. I can define work for you more easily than I can define fun. I do feel some guilt if I'm just doing things for fun. I guess that I'd almost have to define it as frivolous or almost with no work-redeeming value."

Women have the examples of their own mothers and sometimes grandparents who are able to assume many responsibilities. Some grandmothers worked and mothers did not, and conversely some grandmothers did not work, while mothers did. That does not seem to affect the perspective of women who manage work, family, and community responsibilities. These women have been surrounded by diverse examples of the ways in which they can manage their lives, and the primary source of encouragement could come from either earlier generation. Adele came from a family in which the grandparents were an important force. She described her early influences:

> "The most intellectual person in my life was my grandfather. He was a very, very brilliant professor. He gave us a lot of his time and all of his books, so he was the most intellectual person in my life.
> "My mother really set the pace of 'never ever get a B and always be at the top of all of the activities.' She stayed at home and did not have a lot of activities but felt that it was important for me to be active."

We all move into adulthood with the legacy of our past and the learning that comes from experience and from teachings in the family or outside the home.

PRACTICE IN HOME, SCHOOL, AND ACTIVITIES

It seems that in many instances, we are encouraged to assume responsibilities and tasks as a matter of course. We begin by helping with chores in the house—making beds, clearing tables, helping to dust—and learning how to be a daughter, granddaughter, niece, sister, cousin, neighbor. We then learn how to be a student in elementary school and in Sunday school, and the appropriate behavior to use in those settings. Music lessons, afterschool sports, and clubs are added to the list, along with summer camper, pet owner. In every activity there is an intrinsic set of values and behaviors, and we learn these values and behaviors as we become involved in the particular activity.

We learn from observing in the family, by listening to our parents, so that it is relatively easy to know how to be a good daughter or sister. We learn what is important to the other family members through interaction and in the way that little girls learn through playacting. Our imitations of mother and her friends help inculcate proper roles and actions. The doll play is a method by which those actions which are valuable are played back for playmates and quite often for relatives or adult care givers. This means that there is "instant feedback" for the little girls on the way to reenact the roles.

As girls grow into familial roles, their world enlarges, expanding roles and repertoire of behaviors appropriate for each role. Day school and Sunday school behavior are very similar, and though the content of the behavior may vary, the values tend to be reinforcing. American schools are very solidly based on Judeo-Christian values combined with nationalistic values, so there is little conflict between the situations. In addition to learning how to be good pupils, learning subject matter, sitting quietly and following directions, the girls learn how to play group games and cooperate with their peers, learning and obeying the rules of organized games. They learn new skills and modes while easing into transitions between roles. The expectations for a girl are more traditional and stratified than those for a boy, since the girl is expected to conform and be "ladylike." Some women have had the opportunity to be given encouragement by teachers or administrators who recognized their promise or potential.

Those women who have learned to handle multiple roles with relative ease are almost unaware of the starting point in their lives. They can remember the examples in the family or school and the encouragement they received, but they find it difficult to pinpoint the stage of their lives when they began to be busy. When pressed, they remember that they were members of youth organizations, active in church, taking music or dance lessons, and were assuming home responsibilities even in elementary school. One woman said:

"I think there was always a degree of acceptance of
activity in my family. I think my mother was the real
force in encouraging me constantly to move forward
and have a career. My father was an intellectual, and
he pushed that strain in me. But it was my mother who
gave me tremendous reinforcement and pushed me
toward a career and profession. She gave me reinforcement by saying, 'That's what a woman should do.' She
was an organization type, and I often say, in another
generation, she would have been me. I was fulfilling
her life."

The level of activities increases as the girls get older, and
with each increase in activity, they become more and more
proficient at handling many responsibilities, moving from
role to role with ease, without excessive stress.

Contrary to some of the articles written about them,
women are team players or are familiar with the responsibilities associated with membership in an ensemble. Many
women have been active in sports and have learned how to
function on a team in order to win and to work together.
Many of the girls who have taken music or dance lessons
learned how to cooperate to produce pleasant sounds or
pleasing patterns. I think there are some assumptions that
girls' sports or activities are not as demanding or as interesting as those of boys. However, the teamwork and cooperation required has no sex bounds, and a team's primary goal
is to win the game. So girls learn how to work together to
win. Many girls have the experience of being captain as
well. This means that they know the meaning of being a
leader in competition with other groups.

Much is made of the type of play in which girls imitate
mothers and activities within the home, but this is not the
sole type of activity in which girls engage. Granted, little
girls play in twos and threes much of the time, but they are
introduced to team sports and group activities in elementary school, Sunday school, and youth organizations. The
cooperation in this type of activity is not too dissimilar from
the type of cooperation learned within the confines of the

family. Girls are oriented to relationships with others and enjoy the extension of those relationships to other settings. Studies show that girls spend considerable time discussing rules and the correct ways to play games, but they learn how to be team members or leaders in the process. One woman recalled her activities throughout her school years.

"I think that as a child I was very active. Although I certainly wasn't great at everything, I did pursue a number of interests in high school which continued. Actually in junior high school I got involved in a number of activities that were quite diverse. In those days, I was an athlete. I'm not now at all, but I was active in sports. I've always been active in music and at one point thought of becoming a musician. Music has always been an important part of my life and has always, until recent years, taken a great deal of time. I used to practice three and four hours a day; something which to this day, my husband does not understand.

"In high school, I gave up athletics to a certain extent and concentrated more on academics and music but became more eclectic in my musical interests. In college I did very little studying and a lot of activity. I was active in virtually every musical organization on the campus and in student government issues. I became active in dorm politics. I regret a little bit that I did not take as much opportunity to delve into academics. All of this activity came from my parents who were involved in different things and set the pattern for me. I loved school all the way through with minor variations, worked pretty hard, was a reasonably good to excellent student, depending on the year and whether I was in love and how confused I was about what I wanted to do. I normally took extra work and was on a list of committees and choruses and debating societies."

These women who remembered their heavy involvement with activities outside the home also remembered that their families encouraged them and were pleased with their accomplishments. They were made to feel as if they were special and could accomplish everything they set out to accomplish. They were not all from families in which mothers or parents were active, but they were supported in their interests.

VALUES

Not only have these women always been busy, taking on many responsibilities and leading active lives, they have carried out their tasks with a sense of mission. They came from families where standards of excellence were held up for the children, and these standards were dispensed in the guise of sayings such as: "Anything worth doing is worth doing well" or to the contrary, "Not everything worth doing is worth doing well." "To those to whom much is given, much must be returned." These maxims communicated that responsibilities must be carried out with a sense of earnestness, completeness, and be of high quality. Sloppiness and shoddy work, whether in the home or outside, were not to be tolerated, because the quality of the work reflected on the character of the person performing that task.

It has long been an American ideal that the best person is one who is well-rounded. The expectation is that a person will have a commitment to work, to family, to community, to religious activities, and to fun. We decry the "workaholic," the "drudge," the "playboy," because these types lack balance in their lives: they emphasize one part of life to the exclusion of the other aspects. In one sense, women who have been able to handle multiple roles were girls who understood and accepted this American ideal of being well-rounded. They embodied the concept of the All-American Girl. They believe in hard work, service, play, and cooperation and have made these concepts an integral part of their lives from girlhood. They were encouraged, coached, and tutored by parents, grandparents, sympathetic teachers, and youth-group leaders.

Your Own Self-Assessment

Since many women have not thought about their own competencies and abilities to handle multiple roles in relationship to their childhood, I think it is helpful to reassess one's strengths by starting at the beginning. Here are some memory prods that will help you begin the process.

1. List the roles you played in your family as you were growing up.
2. Sketch the behaviors associated with each role and with the person who taught you how to behave.
3. List the activities you engaged in between the ages of eight and eighteen.
4. What were some of the skills you learned through participation in those activities?
5. Who were the people who helped you learn those skills?
6. What are some of those youthful skills you are still using?

The purpose of this exercise is to help you begin to understand some of the characteristics you possess that can help you manage your many roles and responsibilities.

WOMEN'S CHARACTERISTICS

Many of the traditional ideas and stereotypes about women and their roles obscure and denigrate the basic worth of women. The stereotypes tend to perpetuate ideas that women are incompetent, stupid, disorganized, and uninterested in their environment. Of course, in every stereotype there is a germ of reality, but it deprives the object of the stereotype of dignity and provides the other with a false sense of superiority. So the myths and stereotypes about women provide a false sense of superiority for men while diminishing both sexes.

The radical spokeswomen of the movement for women's rights attempted to counter the stereotypes not only by denying them but also by attacking the traditional activities and characteristics of women. They wanted to set right the wrongs inflicted on women and to ensure that women would be granted equity and equality. In so doing, the radicals denied that women were different in any way from men. The idea that the sexes had different characteristics related to function and not to societal status was anathema to them. They therefore rejected any notions that there are values and actions special for women and important to society.

People often go to extremes in social movements. The early proponents develop arguments denying differences between their group and the group in power. They then begin to extol the superior virtues of their own group. There often results a counterreaction or reexamination of the qualities and condition of the group striving for equality.

A reappraisal of women is being done in a quiet way by Jean Baker Miller, Carolyn Heilbrun, and Carol Gilligan, among others. These thoughtful scholars have analyzed many womanly characteristics and behaviors. They have found real differences in the ways in which the sexes approach life and perform in daily existence. The differences can be attributed to women's continuing need for relationships and the high value they place on them. They have interpreted meaningfully women's concern for others and the values associated with nurturing. Consequently, women can begin to understand themselves better and develop a greater appreciation of their inner nature.

Some women wonder whether these characteristics are the consequence of nature or of society. Time could probably be better spent determining how we can function more fully as human beings who happen to be women.

Paradoxically some people concerned about improving the condition of women define equality as being more like men, with women behaving like men: dressing like men, and carrying out policies and programs that have gone unquestioned for generations. We can find in the writings of Miller and Gilligan supportive reasons for resisting the push to turn us into mere copies of the men in society. These scholars are helping us understand that there is value associated with the unique qualities of women.

Other people are equally as earnest about maintaining traditional, conservative views of women in society. Change upsets those people and unsettles their lives. It creates anxiety and demands adjustments. Those of both sexes who resist change often use the Bible to justify their desire to leave roles as they have been. They may cite the book of Genesis as proof that woman is subject to the domination of man. Yet the same book describes the Creation in which "God created man in his own image, in the image of God he created him; male and female, he created them." The story unfolds in Genesis and in other books that woman is to man as is his own body and is to be treated as such. In Ephesians, men are counseled to nourish and cherish their wives as their own flesh, since no man can hate his own flesh. Those who use the Bible as a sourcebook to justify the subordination of women neglect parts of the Christian message: that faith is based on equality before God and that the cross destroys all positions based on power.

Perhaps we should try to reestablish the sense of wonder and excitement that was a part of our lives when we were young girls. These were motivating forces which helped us learn new concepts, assimilate new roles, and acquire skills with which to handle responsibilities. If we relearn these qualities, we can cope with the opportunities open before us.

How should we deal with stereotypes? It will help if we remember that the stereotypes serve a purpose and are designed to portray simplistically a group, women in this instance, as deserving of inferior status. How many women do you know who are dizzy, silly, dumb, fearful, passive, indecisive, uninformed, uninterested in the world, vain, interested only in fashion and cosmetics, weak, weepy, unpunctual, unadventurous, dependent, superstitious, or unmotivated? As I mentioned earlier, there are bits of reality in every stereotype, and they serve to make the group being caricatured feel powerless.

The radical women reformers set about combating stereotypes of women by creating images of women. These images were strident, aggressive, angry, hostile to men, unkempt, ambitious, crusading. These new stereotypes were frightening to many women, but they served to offer alternatives to earlier images. They made men and women rethink the capabilities of women. Eventually the images helped provide confidence to some women who repudiated these "tough" images by achieving a style somewhere in the middle, a style of their own.

How does one find a style that is comfortable and fits? Many women have looked at each phase of life as they did as young girls, with interest, anticipation, curiosity, and commitment. They seek the richness in every situation, searching out new ways to use old skills and new skills for the future. One woman said:

> "I experience some tension between my own human expectations of myself and the demands inherent in my job. Some of those demands are ones which I have imposed, however. I think that some of my greatest satisfactions come from feeling productive. I am fortunate in that I have constantly grown in my work, although I'm always straining at the bit. That's my nature. I'm always impatient and think, O.K., I've learned that trick, what's the next trick? But as I look back on the last five or ten years, I've learned an enormous number of tricks."

Even the routine tasks at home or work can be interesting if they are approached as a challenge and a learning experience, an opportunity to look for more efficient ways of completing the task. Routine chores may be used as windows on the total operation of a function or an office, as a part of creating an environment at home. You can set standards for your performance and continually measure yourself against those standards, whether they concern the time needed or the quality of the work itself.

However, it is important not to become so pleased with the routine that you never look for changes. The routine can be comforting and satisfying because you need not think as you perform the tasks. It is important to keep one's self open to new ideas, insights, ways of doing things, and to the world as it changes. Change is unsettling but exciting. Change is provocative and discomforting because it continually challenges our beliefs and causes us to understand new conditions with reference to enduring values.

Women traditionally have valued relationships within the family and with other people. They have sought to nurture others and to carry that nurturing into the larger society. The occupations and professions most closely identified with women are those dedicated to caring for others and to giving service. These values are unchanging and are often buttressed by a strong religious faith so that women can cope with change. They can handle it because the core of their lives is stable and gives meaning to much that they experience. There is a purposefulness about women. They need not be caught in the stereotypes of the career woman or the housewife because women mix all types of activity in their lives—work, play, and nurturing. The sense of purpose was expressed by an eighty-two-year-old lawyer who is still practicing:

> "Thank God for work. It's the greatest thing in the world. It keeps me young and alive. It has been wonderful for me."

Vitality can be maintained in all aspects of life if the purpose of life is understood and appreciated.

CHAPTER 3

Juggling
and Stretching the Hours

Time is like the weather to Americans. We talk about it continually. People either have too much of it or not enough. Time is bought and sold, and is a valuable commodity. We save it, squander it, and are obsessed with finding ways to use it wisely. Countless technicians spend their working hours trying to devise methods to save time for American businesses and government. Time is an important part of the American society and the American mind, and women are certainly affected by the devotion to and the obligations imposed by time.

Since women are responsible for many tasks and responsibilities in the home and outside, they have to learn how to handle time wisely. They have to use time in ways that stretch the available hours and permit them to have control of their activities. It is a lack of control that causes many women to be distracted and disorganized, thus contributing to stress. Some women have learned how to handle time in such a way that they can manage many, many responsibilities with ease. This ability has been acquired gradually from youth and is often taken for granted. We will explore some of the techniques which these women have devised to help them stay "ahead of time."

There is considerable controversy about the responsibilities assumed by, imposed on, or carried out by women. Some people maintain that women should not have to do more than men, and that multiple responsibilities and roles are a burden and are discriminatory against women. Others believe that women are competent to assume multiple responsibilities and are not discriminated against because they possess a skill not often held by men. Perhaps it is a mixed blessing that women do know from childhood how to handle many roles and responsibilities, but women approach these roles and responsibilities in different ways. Some women do it well and others poorly, and the management of time is one of the key factors in the accomplishment of those tasks.

The majority of working women are concentrated in those industries and sectors of the economy which provide services to clients. Service businesses, as mentioned earlier, provide assistance in the areas of financial and banking matters, hospitality and feeding, governmental, educational, health, and personal services. This is an increasing sector of the American economic life as manufacturing declines, and the country tries to make the transition from an industrialized base to a technological base, from a blue-collar to a white-collar society. The women employed in these businesses and organizations are primarily on the levels of the organization where they work directly with the client. They are the receptionists, bank tellers, clerks, teachers, social workers, keypunch operators, word processor operators, secretaries, administrative assistants. They are the contacts with the public and the "glue" that holds the offices together.

Many of these jobs held by women are based on tradition and they utilize traditional women's skills. The woman of the household is usually the one who greets the guest at the door, as does the receptionist. She takes coats and makes people welcome. She offers and provides refreshments, as do many secretaries and certainly food-service employees. The routine details of offices are quite similar to those of the home and, indeed, are often referred to as "housekeeping details." Order in offices, stores, and other businesses is often the responsibility of women, just as it is in the home.

Women are often given jobs that require a pleasant manner and attention to detail; they are the voices and public faces of many public and private organizations.

The nurturing, mothering qualities of women are the basis of another set of occupations devoted to caring for people. Health services, teaching, recreational services, counseling, psychological and psychiatric services, and social work are occupational areas that require staff who are concerned with and devoted to giving attention to those in need. The intangible characteristics that define the practitioners in these fields are most often those used to define women: warm, loving, caring, helping, responsive, supportive, ministering, nurturant, well-intentioned, helpful, sincere.

In addition to the learned female skills being extended into the world of work, many community organizations and church activities reflect the use of the same skills. Many of these activities preceded the movement of women into the labor force, so that they offered outlets for women to provide service to others in the context of their neighborhood or religious group. The altar guilds, sewing circles, charity groups were the means by which women could come together and do for others. They perceived a need whether in their own church, immediate neighborhood, or in the larger society, and they joined to do something about that need.

Sewing, cooking, serving, cleaning are tasks that can be done and are done in every setting, from tiny home to large organization. Women carry out this work without special orientation or training, and they are comfortable doing these things regardless of the sponsorship. Only recently have women objected to being confined to areas in which these chores were expected. They have wanted to be able to move into a wide range of responsibilities, most of which are not labeled "women's work." However, they carry into new areas of responsibility those womanly characteristics which are learned or inbred, so that the women have the capacity to transform a job to reflect some of those qualities.

One of those qualities is a respect, sometimes a reverence, for time. Some women know how to structure the hours to make them productive and satisfying. It is when this ability is lacking, as mentioned before, that women feel disorganized and disoriented, a sense of being out of control. Most women have had the good fortune to grow up learning how to manage the time available to them.

WOMEN AS TIMEKEEPERS

The skill or ability to be timekeepers is not often recognized or acknowledged by women or by the men in their lives. In fact, our society on the whole tends to underestimate the competence of women to handle time. We have all heard the jokes about women always being late, never on time, always keeping men waiting. Well, if that were truly the case, why would women be given the responsibility to be the timekeepers of America?

The mothers, secretaries, assistants, and organizers are the people who arrange schedules and calendars and monitor the arrangements. It is generally the mother who sets up the social calendar in the home, planning for holidays and family get-togethers. It is she who plans the child's introduction to the school calendar and the necessity of observing the times set by the school authorities. It is the mother who sets the schedule of chores, school, play, and other activities for the children in the family. Problems arise when this timekeeping is not done, problems within the family and with outside authorities, but the responsibility for this control of the calendar is usually assumed to be that of the mother.

It is the mother who usually is responsible for getting the children off to school on time, and it is she who gets the husband off to work on time. She starts the household off each day, taking responsibility for everyone in the family, in addition to getting herself ready to leave for work on time. Not only must she see that her family is on time but she has to teach good habits and consciousness of time as the children grow to have increasing responsibility. Her goal is to have each member of the family learn attitudes that contribute to punctuality and the ability to plan and handle time sensibly.

In most executive suites and managers' offices, there is a secretary or an assistant who has the job of handling the boss's appointment calendar. It is she who controls his comings and goings, who sees how he functions and when, how relaxed or frenetic his day will be, and where he will be at what time. Very few people, executive or secretary, understand the potential power of this job, because the schedule and the ability of the executive to handle that schedule can make or break him or her. The pacing of the day—which alternates activities and levels of decisions, types of people and problems—is crucial in maintaining control of one's job and senses. Very few executives take time to analyze the style of work or the energy level and fatigue factors inherent in any job and the need to adjust the schedule to those factors. However, it is women who are entrusted with handling this very important part of the economic and political life of the country. No group of people with a poor understanding of time could be entrusted with handling such an important responsibility, so the jokes serve to obscure the reality of women's competence.

Dorothy is the secretary of an executive in a middle-sized company that provides financial services and money management and investments to small investors. Dottie's boss must contact potential clients, counsel current clients, participate in company-management meetings, participate in Chamber of Commerce activities and professional groups. When she was hired, one phrase in the job description read, "Must schedule appointments and arrange calendar." The general range of activities was sketched out for her. For a while after she started, she reviewed each of the requests, meeting announcements, and invitations with her boss.

Now she understands the nature of his responsibilities and his work style well enough that she has full control over his professional calendar. At the end of each day, she reviews the plan for the next day and gives him a small card with typed agenda. At the end of each week, she gives him a typed schedule for the following week. Dottie not only arranges the timetable but she sees to it that he keeps to the schedule and is on time for each event. She ushers people into his office and then ensures that they do not overstay by discreetly notifying her boss that the next appointment is imminent. She functions as the guardian of the hours, guaranteeing that her boss looks good and is productive.

Those women who act as timekeepers for other people keep the clocks of commerce going, by opening and closing the offices, stores, and organizations. They are the guides by which everyone knows that all is well and in order to conduct business. Most observers of the behavior of women workers comment on their ability to punch the clock on time. They do not misplace their sense of time when they go on breaks or to lunch, and they return to their work stations at the expected time. They also display a keen sense of time when the closing hour approaches, and they depart with great punctuality. This is not because of lack of loyalty or of devotion to duty, but because they must scurry home to take care of other duties.

This time sense and type of response to obligations of time is not dependent on or affected by marital status. It applies to married women, women with families, and single women. They know how to use time and how many activities to pack into a twenty-four-hour period. Let us examine some of the ways in which this is done.

THE TIMING OF MOTHERHOOD

Lydia in her mid-twenties is immersed in her first job. She is in the marketing department of a chain store with a strong blue-collar suburban base. She had two years of college before she started working, is continuing her education at night, and takes occasional courses on weekends. She lived at home when she graduated from high school and during her time at the community college, but she now shares an apartment with two other young women.

Lydia's job is considered to be semiprofessional, halfway between clerical and professional. She helps prepare copy for newspaper advertisements, makes contact with departments for information on merchandise and prices, and works with comparable advertising personnel on newspaper staffs. She sometimes works with the technical staff who prepare the copy for printing, and she finds the job a fascinating window on the world of advertising and retail business. She is studying business administration with a concentration in marketing and hopes to be promoted to a copywriter and supervisor when she obtains her degree. The company might give her scholarship assistance after she completes five years of employment. She has another year before she is eligible to compete for a scholarship.

Although work fills the major part of Lydia's life, there are other things she does to give her a sense of completeness. She and her roommates join another set of roommates to bowl once a week; they are part of a league in their neighborhood. Lydia's classes take two nights a week, and study is usually done on the weekend and on one other weeknight. She will go on occasion to a folk dance at the local high school if one of her friends is going. She shops on Saturdays or on a free evening, and chores around the apartment are sandwiched into the weekend or evenings. When she has time, she goes to her parents' home for Sunday dinner and a visit. Holidays are spent with the family and are opportunities to renew high school friendships and see childhood friends at church.

The major lament Lydia has is that she has so little time to do some of the things she would like to do: see more movies, read books, keep closer ties with old friends, explore the city, learn about art and music, and maybe take a crafts class. She sometimes wonders what she will do in the future and whether she should think about marriage and motherhood. However, she laughs about the prospect, since she has no serious male relationships. Her dates are usually in groups, and she is not very concerned about finding a boyfriend. She is enjoying her life as it is unfolding. Her family does not pressure her to get married, and few of her friends are married. Her immediate plans center around getting a college degree and a promotion.

There are millions of American women similar to Lydia, leading busy, contented, productive lives, and feeling somewhat hazy about the future. Some of them give more serious attention to the question of motherhood as they move into their thirties, and it may be an agonizing or an easy question to resolve. The question of becoming a mother can be resolved in vastly different ways, since the resolution is a personal one, though it has societal implications.

There seem to be several major ways of approaching the issue of the timing for marriage and parenting. The considerations of the biological clock, the tugs of ambition, and career mobility are factors in these decisions, though there are many factors in each individual case that should be considered.

Postponement of career or work is one option available to women. Under this option, the couple marry and begin their family. They may have one or several children, but the mother spends the early years of the marriage devoting her time to rearing the preschool child or children. The father concentrates his efforts on his job and getting a grasp of the requirements of the company and the occupational area.

On the other hand, both husband and wife can work at the beginning of the marriage and determine a set number of years before they will have children or put off having children until some unspecified time. They can get established at work and begin to accrue savings for a permanent residence and furnishings and the future. Their relationship will have time to become fairly well established, and there are some couples who determine during this time that

Roles

they do not want to have a family and others who find that they cannot.

There are some women who decide that they do not want to make the commitment to marriage but that they can live fully as a single person. They find that they make this choice in spite of pressures to the contrary and that life need not be lived as on Noah's ark. Many of these women do not talk of making a permanent vow to be single but of leaving the option open to marry, if they so desire, at some future time. One woman described her decision in this way:

> "One of the most important questions I had to deal with was what would I do in the future. I could feel the outside pressure in some ways, from friends, from my mother. I'll be frank. I thought I would be doing a disservice to myself if I didn't concentrate on my job and on trying to advance myself. I decided that I would do what I did well and think about moving ahead. I wanted to decide for myself and take control of my life. This is the option I have chosen, for now."

There is also the option of working before and after marriage and having children without taking any major breaks in one's work life. Most large and even small employers have provisions for maternity leave, so that a woman can take a specified period of time out to prepare for, give birth to, and settle in with the newborn before returning to work. Many women choose this option, not out of a deep-felt need to be a part of the work force, but out of financial necessity or excess energy which is not absorbed by care of a baby. However, they must face the difficult problem of finding adequate care for the baby while they are at work.

Within these three general patterns, there are many available options tailored to each woman and her partner, if the matter is one of determining to have a family and the appropriate timing. These decisions cannot be made alone, and one of the characteristics of women is that they do relate to others and function in a cooperative mode, relying on the relationship to help sustain them. Decisions about one's future are so important that the modern woman should consider all the options and how the outcome of each would fit her and her loved ones. She should include her husband, her close siblings or parents, and close friends in the process so that she has an opportunity to hear many different opinions, and the resolution should be mutually determined with her spouse.

When one is in the process of making life choices, external support is needed to alleviate the loneliness felt by one person or two persons seeking to make decisions, some of which will be irrevocable. The contradictory evidence on medical and biological effects of early or later parenting should be considered, along with the moral and ethical implications of determining when marriage and a family might be appropriate. The counsel of professionals can be sought as there are often unresolved simmering issues brought into a relationship from the families of the couple's childhoods. A professional counselor, therapist, or minister can help the couple understand what some of the issues are so that they can begin to resolve them in their own fashion. There may be times when group counseling is recommended so that the couple can discuss their problems or review their quandaries with couples facing the same issues.

Lydia and her friends are fortunate, because they are free to explore their options in an era that is more relaxed than a generation earlier. Her mother had fewer options, since the expectation was that she would get married, work for a while, but devote the bulk of her time and energy to home and children. Lydia is not being pressured to make decisions before she is ready to do so. Our era is a benign one because a generation of women have worked hard and pushed the frontiers so that Lydia's generation can have the time to determine what they can do outside the family walls. They bring a sense of earned independence to a mature relationship.

TECHNIQUES AND METHODS
OF MANAGING TIME

The independence and the explored options are possible because these young women have learned how to manipulate time and responsibilities and are refining and adding to that knowledge every day. Lydia's schedule sounds extremely busy, but there are millions of women with similar schedules and millions of others who are even busier. There are women who work, have children, take classes, volunteer in church and community, and have social activities as well.

How do they have time? There are many techniques that women have devised to help them accomplish diverse responsibilities. Some of these methods are ones the women have created consciously and others have developed without any thought or prior planning.

Make Lists and Inventories

Innumerable women do plan for the short-term tasks and long-term goals, and they use paper and more paper on which to do this planning. Making lists is the most common way to plan for the short term. Many women make a list of every item that they must accomplish on a given day. Others have several lists—one for home, one for work, one for things to be done while in transit from home to work and vice versa. Others sit down to do this at the beginning of the week or at the end of the week; it is the sitting down regularly and making a weekly list that is important. They list the important goals for the week, such as finishing a sewing project or writing a sales campaign prospectus. Then they divide up the week by days and make lists for each day. The most frequent complaint from list makers is that they have slips of paper in every pocket and purse.

There are many women who plan their schedule and activities in their heads and do not use the device of writing anything down. This is essentially true of the women who plan for the more distant future; they carry around the plans in their heads. They often do not put the plans in effect, because they do not think through the methods by which they can achieve those goals.

Writing out what has to be is a good way of conducting an inventory and determining if there are too many things on the list and if they are realistic chores or burdens. Periodically, you might try this exercise as a way of making an inventory of your activities, using these headings or some of your own: To Be Done; How; Purpose; Effect in Five Years.

You would enter each task in the "To Be Done" column. In the "How" column, you would write a short description of the way in which you would expect to accomplish this task. The third column is very important, because it will help you determine if the activity or task is "busy work" or has meaning for you or others. Carefully and honestly think through the reason for doing the task. Does it contribute to your physical well-being? Does it enhance your personal environment and make it more pleasant? Does it help others? Does it make you feel good? Does it help you on the job? Does it contribute to better relationships at home? Is this task necessary, or is it a time-filler? Each task will have a purpose which only you can determine. The answers in the "Purpose" column and in the "Effect" column will help you begin to sort out the trivial and meaningless from the necessary and growth-enhancing.

Why would anyone want to examine a chore as mundane as, for example, painting a kitchen? Because examination will help you place the chore in perspective and help you find a sense of balance. Painting the kitchen may not be a wonderful chore, but may contribute to a cleaner, more pleasant environment to work in and be in. The finished kitchen may lift your spirits, give you a brighter attitude at work and with family, or may contribute to the value of the property. However, the overall impact of painting the kitchen cannot be analyzed in isolation; it must be looked at in the context of all the other tasks. It may be that the kitchen-painting project should be postponed because it may create stress for you and others around you.

You should not waste time conducting an inventory on a regular basis. This is a helpful exercise at those times when you begin to feel that the world is falling in on you and that you have entirely too much to do. It is at those times that a pencil and paper and a period of quiet introspection have been helpful to many women. They have had an opportunity to look at themselves in relationship to the things they want to accomplish and the reasons they are doing them and what the effects will be for themselves and for others. They can begin to take a long view by separating themselves from the frenzy of the immediate.

SLEEP LESS

A frequent strategy is to decrease the number of hours spent sleeping. One woman described the way she got all her work done.

> "I get up at 5:00 in the morning for a variety of reasons. That is my time. It is quiet and gives me a chance to get a head start. I am extremely organized and don't function well in clutter, so the extra time in the morning gives me a chance to clean up the clutter in the house and in my head. I am always thinking, from the time I wake up until I go to bed. So, by getting up early, I can use the time to get organized."

Many women have made the decision that they can give up an hour at either end of the day and make it productive time.

DO MECHANICAL REPAIRS

Some working women have decided that one of the ways they can save time or use it more effectively is by becoming mechanics. One young woman was in despair that her car was costing increasing amounts of money for repairs, towing, and her own time off from work. She went to evening school and took two semesters of auto mechanics, using her own auto in the hands-on sessions. As a result, she can do minor repairs herself, and, more important, she can diagnose some of the troubles with the car and tell the garage what needs to be done. Her bills have diminished, as has her time away from the office, and her self-confidence has grown. Her brother is now in awe of her knowledge of cars and asks for her advice.

Another woman reported:

> "I learned how to do appliance repairs, how to service the dishwasher and washing machine. I found that it is not too difficult, and the repairmen were cooperative. I asked them to show me how to fix the small problems and they did. Each time one of them would come—the disposal repairman, the washing machine repairman, the dishwasher repairman, the television man—I would ask him to teach me. I found that it was easier to do the repairs myself than stand around waiting for them to show up. I have a great sense of pride in fixing those things. I didn't need to take on any additional things, but it had to be. In fact, I changed my first tire the other day because I couldn't get anyone to come and do it. I was really angry, but it only took me twenty minutes. Then I felt foolish, and wondered why I hadn't tried doing it myself before."

SIMPLIFY YOUR LIFE

There are other women who have found that they need to simplify their lives in order to accomplish everything on their lists. Some of the ways they have done this are: meal preparation, cooking the dinner entrées on the weekend and freezing them; making all the lunches on the weekend and freezing them; eating dinners out many nights; buying take-out dinners; buying foodstocks and assigning to children some cooking chores; hiring a housekeeper to clean and prepare meals; sharing cooking with another single-parent family; using commercial frozen meals; using microwave ovens and/or slow cookers.

One woman found that she had more time if she moved her residence closer to her office. She then did not have to commute. This is not possible in many cities, but flexible work hours have helped some women handle the crush of tedious commuting. Their work schedule is such that they do not have to come and go at the same hours that the majority of workers are on the road or on the trains.

Many women talk about learning to ignore dirt. One woman spoke of getting exercise by picking up dust balls as she walked around her house, but she expressed dismay because she could not have a spotless house. However, she said:

> "Liberation was a shiny house. I used to really want a shiny house. A lot of me was tied up in that, and it was the first breakthrough that I had about twenty years ago, and the rest has been easy since then. My mother always kept and still does keep a perfect house; she spends a lot of time waxing floors. Now I don't think that I will ever be able to get over coming into my dirty house, because I find myself wishing it were clean. Cleanliness allows me to relax more, because that's the kind of house I was raised in. I think my daughter will have a much easier time feeling comfortable in a disorderly house. I am never going to be comfortable, but I realized a long time ago that I was not going to put the time into it that my mother does. But I can't get over that feeling of discomfort when guests discover dust balls and toothpaste on the sink."

GET HELP WITH CHORES

Then there are many women who incorporate their families, including children, into the chores. If they live alone, they may work out cooperative plans with friends to accomplish major cleaning or painting projects. Women who insist that family members participate in household chores, errands, and other responsibilities tend to be less burdened by actual physical fatigue. The sharing should begin when the mother begins to work or when the chil-

dren are quite young. There will be a sense of pride that
everyone in the household is contributing to the well-being
of the family, and husbands can certainly do all the things
that a woman can do: dusting, mopping, shopping, cooking.

Work parties can be organized by groups of friends or
work colleagues. This is often done when a friend is
moving, but is done less often for heavy cleaning or
painting projects. This could be the occasion for a day of fun
for unmarried people and a way to take care of some of the
more extensive cleaning projects that cannot normally be
handled by one person.

Of course, if a woman has the financial means, she can
pay someone to take care of the cleaning, washing and
ironing, and errands. There are many women who do not
have large incomes, but they have chosen to pay someone
to clean for them once or twice a month. This is one way to
buy time, the most valuable commodity available to a
working woman. Many of the women who hire cleaning
help trade off a consumer purchase as they balance their
budgets. There is a sense of satisfaction that comes from
walking into a clean house or apartment, a sense of being
cared for if the work has been done by others. Fantasy or
wish fulfillment of this small magnitude sometimes helps
balance the stress associated with multiple roles.

Making a trade-off, buying cleaning service instead of a
new dress, makes you feel better and allows you time to do
something that couldn't be done otherwise. On the other
hand, there are women who enjoy the challenge of doing
their own housework. They feel that it gives them exercise
they don't get on their paid jobs, and they enjoy the sense of
accomplishment from completing the polishing and mopping, something they do not often do in their work lives.
There are some women who say they can take out their
frustrations and hostilities on the floors and windows so
that they feel better when they are finished.

There are increasing numbers of single-parent families
headed by mothers, and these women find that they have to
make compromises on their standard of living, along with

their standard of cleanliness. Some of them feel as this mother does:

> "There are all sorts of arrangements that you can make for the children and the house, but the children's needs are infinite. You have to meet them in some degree, you can't write them off. You can't say, I'll let the children go in unclean jeans. So you starch everything, because you can't fail to deal with the children as they need your help. That kind of juggling and that kind of burden is much greater for many of us than it used to be."

For many of these families, it is extremely necessary to have the children assume part of the responsibility for chores. They not only will be able to contribute to their own well-being, they are also part of a cooperative effort. They can be helped to mature in a constructive manner, being concerned for others and learning to give of themselves, even if only their time and physical energy. This does not mean that children should be deprived of their childhood by being given undue responsibility, total care of the house or siblings. It means that they should take on responsibilities suitable to their age, strength, and ability. If a family work well together, there is less stress. The mother can be head of the household only if she too is disciplined and assumes her role as the wise and just leader of the family. She cannot abdicate and be another member of the family. She must be the one upon whose shoulders rests the mantle of responsibility, but the mantle will be lighter if she is willing to teach her children how to carry part of the burden.

CONSERVE ENERGY

Time can be saved by organizing tasks, by getting the help of other people, by figuring out efficient methods, and by conserving one's energy. Many women run continually from one place to another, from one task to another, never reaching their destination, never completing anything.

They expend considerable amounts of energy and have very little to show for their time and activity. Many women have almost no idea of their own physical and mental reserves and how much they are capable of accomplishing. Now, women who handle multiple roles well have found that it requires considerable self-understanding and knowledge. They become conscious of the amount of sleep they need and how many hours of work cause them to feel fatigue and to operate below their "feel good" level. They are conscious of how much driving or walking they can do before they feel tired. They know how long they can stand on their feet or how many rooms they can vacuum before they feel pooped. They know how many evening meetings they can attend or how many interrupted phone conversations they can conduct before feeling jangled. They become aware of how many hours of work they can put in before needing a respite of some type, reading a magazine, going to a movie, gossiping about fashions. In short, they learn to gauge their own capacity so that they can expend their energy in a meaningful way.

Some women find that they can conserve their energy and also save time by planning their errands. They chart the trips that must be taken during the week: to the cleaners, to the shoe repair shop, to the grocery, to the hardware, to the library, to buy clothes, to pick up and deliver children, and on and on. They estimate which errands can be accomplished to and from work, in the evenings, and which must be saved for weekends or work holidays. They figure out which errands can be grouped together because of geographic proximity and the time involved with each. In this way, they can conserve time, energy, and fuel, and they do not run hither and thither without accomplishing some errand.

This discussion may sound trivial and unnecessary, but many women do not take the time to consider the small aspects of their lives. It is those parts which can defeat a woman and make her life seem chaotic and aimless, overwhelming her to the point where she is not able to cope with any part of her life. As one woman said about her methods: "You have to be organized to use time to its fullest. Energy is important, but organization is the thing. You cannot treat anything as unimportant, because it's the sum of all the small unimportant things that adds up to doing a good job."

INSIGHTS FROM OLDER WOMEN'S EXPERIENCE

Most women learn by bumbling through, working out solutions to their hectic schedules, occasionally glancing at an article they think will give them new insights, occasionally picking up a suggestion from a friend. There are few opportunities to explore options for handling multiple responsibilities, and the older women who shared their ideas with me were grateful to have a chance to review some of their methods for coping. As they talked of the ways in which they had combined their many roles, or perhaps reconciled those roles, a pattern emerged.

They had developed a style that helped them, but the style evolved over the years. As young women, they did not think about their activities, they just did them, often paying a high price in relationships or energy. Later, they began to set priorities for their lives. One successful executive remembered: "As a young woman, I was bedazzled with the possibilities before me. Then I was utterly frustrated by the demands placed upon me and the speed at which life moved. I am not sure that I slowed down, but I learned to pace myself."

How does one pace oneself? One woman in her late fifties said:

> "I used to feel a lot more stress because I allowed myself to think that half the world was depending on me. I think that false responsibilities create the greatest strain, and the relief comes when you can separate

false from true. That is very important. We assume
false assumptions and then we take certain pleasure in
that assumption. Once I came to terms with my own
confidence and limited my perspective to my real
world and the people in that world, I could handle
things more easily."

The pacing of your life is tied to accepting life for what it is
and yourself for who you are, not forgoing the dreams or
ambitions, the hopes of achieving your goals. It is a realization that much of the stress and strain is self-imposed and is
not from external sources. As one woman explained:

"There is even stress if one has to go to bed before
everything is done, or there is stress because you
didn't do something as well as you could have or
might have done. People put those stresses on themselves even though outside forces are there. I guess
that I decided that those were the stresses which I was
not going to take; I didn't want them. I'm not going to
have the best-looking kitchen or living room, and I'm
not unhappy about it. I decided not to put all my eggs
in one basket. You have multiple roles, and if things in
your life don't always go perfectly in every basket,
well, fortunately things in your life don't go dreadfully
in every basket. So, women can derive pleasure from
more than one source. It doesn't have to be just your
home or garden, but things at work. These things are
the rewards of multiple roles, and that's why I chose
them and want them. I think it's unfortunate that we
don't have the possibility of the rewards that women
have been able to get from many sources."

The older a woman is, the longer she has had to practice
her many skills in different settings. She has acquired
insights about her own abilities and the sources of pleasure
in her everyday life. Many of these pleasures are very
simple ones which go to make full and complete lives. A
never-married woman in her middle years described her
feelings about multiple roles:

"I think just being able to accomplish many activities gives a certain amount of satisfaction. I think that if I were to play only the private life and not have the work life, the recognition would be missed, the ability or opportunity to use organizational talents, the management talents, even growing with people. I would probably look for ways of doing that. I think that cooking a good meal occasionally is a good reward, because I like to cook and don't often have time. I have some warm friends who are completely away from my work, and that's very satisfying. It keeps me from being wrapped up in myself, so the mix of friends and work have been a darn good combination for me."

Women who have balanced multiple roles for four, five, or more decades do so without thinking of many things. They take for granted many of the methods they use because those methods have become a part of the women's unconscious style of handling life. They without much effort utilize the time available and do what they have to do. They function within the context of values, family, and community, and find satisfactions in many things. Often these women were the first in their family to work while raising children, and often they were pioneers in the work force. Many of their female friends and neighbors were home, and some of these women worked because of financial necessity and some, as one woman commented, worked because of "biological necessity," something inside them.

The older women have handled multiple roles in a variety of ways, but they found ways that evolved over years and were generally unplanned. The central focus has been on being independent: learning how to express an inner need for action, channeling energies and intelligence in constructive ways, nurturing family and colleagues, and enjoying their lives. Many of them achieved more than they set out to achieve, at work or in their personal lives, and most of them would not choose to do anything else with their lives if given a choice. They feel that they have been true to the core of their innermost nature and that they have in some way fulfilled their lives. They contradict the common myth that a woman has to make a choice between home and work. They have experienced all the stresses and strains, none deny that, and they have weathered them. They make the assessment that they have had interesting lives, have found excitement and satisfactions, and have learned what is important.

Time is a tool and something that should be used to help women fulfill their potential. However, it is up to each of us to ascertain what that potential is and what our goals are. We can do this by stretching beyond our immediate situation and self. We can do it by determining what is important to us and what motivates our planning and our strategies.

In some ways, the discussion above is very sterile because it focuses on individual women and the ways they have found to handle complex relationships with people and responsibilities. In fact, not one of the women whom I interviewed would ever describe her life or accomplishments as a sole venture. Each woman was a part of a group, family and communal. This is very much an integral part of the way in which women function in all phases of their lives. They are not alone. They fulfill their desires, ambitions, and needs along with others. They are pulled by commitments to their loved ones and to those to whom they feel a sense of responsibility.

The women who manage multiple roles do so, not in a vacuum, but in the context of those who taught them to care and to be competent and of those who need them. They have learned to provide for those needs in a variety of ways at the same time that they are attempting to define their own sense of personhood. They have moved beyond the superficial conformity to a stereotype of what a woman is supposed to be and do. They are acting out their own faith and value with a sense of self-confidence that they can make choices and fulfill their definition of destiny.

CHAPTER 4

Coping with Stress

As women with many roles and many demands upon us, we all face stress and tension. While stress can add excitement and interest to our lives, too often it becomes a problem. With what seems far too much to do, many women face conflict and even mental anguish. Stress may cause headaches, backaches, and other physical pain.

Although discussing stress has become fashionable, nevertheless stress is a real issue for busy women. Stress, as described by individual women, may be related to a variety of different feelings. Some women feel that their roles are in conflict. Others feel pressure about the quality of their work—from others or from themselves. Others experience insecurity about their own competence or about their own choices and priorities.

Some sources of stress are outside us. Most of us wonder whether our own lives measure up to those we are told "have it all." Could we be richer, more glamorous, more powerful, more sexy, and generally more successful? Most of us feel bad that we do not conform to some unrealistic images from television or other media. Some women who need to work feel uncomfortable with idealized images of women who stay home fulfilling traditional women's roles. Other working women, doing necessary but routine jobs, feel bad when confronted with idealized images of working women who accomplish wonderful things. Increasingly, women in the home feel bad about the image that only jobholders find glamorous self-fulfillment. While the media have a positive role in helping us learn options, we must carefully choose what fits ourselves. We must learn to disregard what is unrealistic, and keep down stress from external sources.

Internally, women place themselves under considerable stress. Most important, women set high standards for themselves and try hard to live up to them. Accordingly, they must work hard to maintain self-confidence and a sense of competency.

Many women talk of enjoying praise from co-workers, bosses, or family for doing something well, but acknowledge that it matters less than their own appraisal. Women worry about their ability to do a job well and come up to their standard of excellence, and they are harder on themselves than they are on others. As one woman expressed it: "Everything I do is done with 300 percent of myself in it. I can't settle for less, and it has to be top quality or I'm unhappy. I know that this is silly, but it doesn't matter what anyone else says. I have to do it my way and be the judge."

Other women are troubled by related expectations of themselves. They express feelings of anxiety in trying to accomplish everything that has to be done, whether getting a washing machine repaired or completing a report. They set deadlines that may not be realistic and worry about them until they are met. They feel guilty about not seeing friends as often as they would like or not taking their children out as often as they would like. They feel bad about dust balls, unironed clothes, or unread books. They wonder if they are living life to the fullest or if there is a better way to live. They worry about the way they look, the amount of sleep or exercise they get. There seem to be constant little, or big, nagging problems in their lives.

Too often an individual woman experiences stress, and worries that she is the only one who has these kinds of problems. Actually, comparing experiences with other women can be very reassuring. This kind of sharing is one of the valuable outcomes of the consciousness-raising sessions of the women's movement. In fact, no woman should feel she alone copes with new problems and situations. Much is known about stress and ways of dealing with it.

One significant fact about stress is that it often varies in intensity with age. Younger women, unmarried or childless and at the beginning of their work careers, tend to feel less stress than do women in the midst of child-rearing. Then those women who are in their fifties and sixties feel even less pressure, which suggests that stress is experienced on a curve. Youth and maturity are the low ends, and the zenith is reached during the years with the heaviest family responsibilities.

Even at busy times of life there are many ways women can cope with the stress that comes from maintaining work—of whatever sort—family, and personal life. We all can control and manage time to some degree, as discussed earlier. Equally important for maintaining our vitality are supportive relationships and solitary activities.

RELATIONSHIPS

Women who manage multiple roles well and still manage stress are able to do so for many reasons. Uppermost is an ability to have relationships with others. Close associations not only nurture the women involved but sustain and cushion them from many potentially destructive blows. Women use these relationships for a safe harbor as well as for a source of revitalization. They need and utilize their immediate family as well as friends, particularly women friends.

The lone male is a symbol of the American folk hero. The man who rides into town and rights the wrongs before he rides into the sunset, alone. The man at the top is usually depicted as alone, and tracts are written about the pressures and loneliness of the leader. This image does arise from the national tradition of individualism, but it may work to the disadvantage of our society as a whole in the late twentieth century.

Women, as discussed earlier, often have a supportive, cooperative perspective on life and the world in which they live. This perspective can be described in one instance:

> "Often in an organization, there is a competent person, most often a woman, who clearly feels a sense of obligation both to the purpose of the organization and to the other workers. If you are that person and other people recognize those qualities, there will be a lot of people expressing needs, and not just professional. They come for support, for ideas, for nurturing, and for help in dealing with problems. Some women demonstrate that we care for people, so we are willing to span the boundary between personal and work problems. Your own self-concept and your own personality generate momentum so that other people respond to those parts of you which reach out to them."

For women, this reciprocal aspect of relationships is very important. It is not sufficient to be a care giver, to provide nurture and aid to the distressed. Women want to connect with the other person in a meaningful way. Women give, but they must receive in order to feel confirmed in themselves. They exist with and for those who are a part of their lives.

The women whom I have interviewed and have worked with disassociate themselves from the loner. They, to a woman, assert that they could not carry through their many responsibilities if they did not have the support and caring of others.

WITHIN THE FAMILY

ORIGINAL FAMILY

A very important group of people who provide comfort and support to a woman with multiple roles is the family into which she was born.

Families today tend to be scattered across the country. Social mobility and the search for opportunity caused much of the geographic separation. Since many women have followed their careers or husbands, they have relocated at a distance from their place of origin. However, despite the cost of travel and telephone, families can stay in touch and share their heritage. The American Bicentennial and the publication of Alex Haley's book *Roots* contributed to making many people aware that a partial solution to alienation and the need for identity in an impersonal society was drawing closer to the family and understanding who they have been.

Many women who are not married find that they need the continual contact and encouragement of the family that nurtured them in youth. They may live at a distance, but telephone calls and frequent visits help them maintain a sense of reality about themselves. Often with parents there can be problems if the younger family members are always cast in the role of children. Firmness and a clear sense of self can be important. Brothers and sisters can be strong supporters—some of the best friends a woman can have.

Single women with children find that their family provides them and the children with a sense of stability and continuity. The children know that they are not alone with a separated parent. Even if the grandparents, uncles, aunts, and cousins do not understand the situation or are unhappy about it, they will communicate a sense of love and caring to the children.

This sense of love supports the woman who has many responsibilities. This group of people will usually appreci-

ate her capabilities and will accept her without undue
criticism. Parents keenly appreciate the woman's accomplishments since they contributed to creating this competent woman.

HUSBANDS

Many of the women handling multiple roles do so with
the assistance and support of husbands. And then there are
many who do so in spite of their husbands. Let's talk about
the differences and the effects on the women involved, first
the problems and then the opportunities.

Age often influences the ways in which husbands per-
ceive women's roles. Men's views depend partly on the
ideas of society at the time they became adult and on their
own mother's views. Older men in their fifties and sixties
tend to be more conventional about the expectations for
their wives and for women in general. Many of the women
of that age express the difficulties they faced, in some
instances opposition. Many of the men could not understand their wives' interest in being more than a housewife.
Returning to college for undergraduate or graduate education, or taking on a volunteer or part-time job and then a
full-time job, caused puzzlement and sometimes anger.
Some of the men felt that the change in pattern was an
expression of hostility, defiance of convention, and perhaps
lack of confidence in their own ability to provide for the
needs of the family. Even some men who welcomed the
additional income for the family budget found that they
could not feel easy about a working wife.

Many women recount experiences that are similar. Flor-
ence said:

> "Matt's business kept getting harder and harder, tak-
> ing more and more of his time. I helped in the office a
> few afternoons a week—taking the telephone, typing
> up correspondence, and putting order in the office. As
> things got better, he finally decided to hire a full-time
> secretary so that I could stay home. Yet I found that I

liked working, and the house and kids didn't suffer. I
saw an ad in the local paper advertising for a Girl
Friday, and I applied. The salary was good, and it was
not far from home. Now I left home after Matt and the
kids and got home well before he did. However, my
husband became more and more difficult, trying to get
me to stay home and take care of him. I couldn't and
wouldn't, so there was more and more tension and
strain. The kids finally made me see that the house
was too full of tears and sorrow, and I have not felt any
real stress since we divorced."

Some of the women who have gone through divorce
attribute part of the problem to the changes in their attitudes, interests, and an unfolding of their talents. They
maintain that the husband was not prepared for changes
and could not cope with a wife who was different from the
"girl" he married. However, a working second wife often
did not present problems.

A more common sentiment was voiced by the wife of a
professional man when she talked of the greatest source of
stress in a marriage of more than thirty years.

"I think that there are stresses and strains in my
relationship with Walter, some related to multiple
roles. He has a tendency to say, as children do, 'You're
never home; always away.' When I check the calendar, I usually find that it is something like four times
in four months. He has that feeling a lot, and he may
be out two evenings in every week for four weeks."

In addition to the time away from the family and the
house, there is another problem that confronts some wom-
en. Their spouses do not know how to cope with a successful wife and hope they never will have to. Husbands may
have difficulty facing the fact that they are married to an
achiever. Women reported the stresses of achieving outside
the home and downplaying it for an insecure husband.
Some handle the problem by not talking about their successes, obscuring promotions and salary increases or keeping the husband away from any work-related events. In

some instances, time helped the husband assimilate and accept the wife's achievements.

The most common and frequent complaint and lament of many married women is that their husbands do not help in any way with the household or the children. This is also a source of conflict and argument in many families, particularly when the husband considers the house and the children to be the responsibility of the wife, regardless of the nature of her job or the number of hours she works. One extreme case was that of a woman whose husband worked at home but would not do anything except make his lunch and show repairmen what needed attention. One exasperated wife finally figured out that she was extremely fatigued by the extra burden of the household chores that she and the children were carrying alone. She issued an ultimatum to her husband, who decided to leave home. The former wife admitted that she and the children have now less work since the messiest member of the household is gone.

Husbands, however, can be very helpful and supportive—when properly taught. Millions of women have shown their husbands how to clean, care for the house, and cook. Madeline explained:

> "I have a second strategy, other than planning. It is to push Andy into areas in which he was not comfortable at first. He didn't see the house as his territory. He still looks back at our earlier life as a period of ease. I plan the calendar and schedule him to do things like taking the kids to the dentist and taking care of work in the house. I take the responsibility for keeping track of things, but I also call upon him in a way that tries to push him. I help him see that these chores are unavoidable and that he has to take on certain responsibilities. So far, so good."

Many women gradually phase their husbands and children into doing the chores that have to be done. This is possible primarily because there is an atmosphere of caring and support for one another. Some of the women who regretfully ended a marriage are able to attribute part of the problem to the husband and wife maturing in different directions. Those women who have remarried sometimes have relationships that are very different from the first marriage. Then, of course, there are other women who have not remarried and are not sure they ever will, and their children assume even greater importance to their lives.

Many women reported that their husbands encouraged them to return to school for further education or specialized training. Some women were not confident that they could handle the rigors of course work in their maturity, and the husbands helped them gain a sense of their competence and self-worth. Many of these men encouraged them to find employment and have acted as mentors, telling them how to move through the tangles of work relationships. Barbara mused about her husband of twenty-eight years and his influence:

> "He encouraged me to go to school part time when our son was an infant. He felt that it would be easier for me, and it was. We had to maintain our privacy though, because both our families wanted to get involved and tell us what to do. I think that it was during that period that my husband became my best friend. We worked out whatever our problems were even though in the first ten years of marriage, I could have divorced him easily twenty-six times. But we shared and came through it, and he kept pushing me to do those things which would make use of my talents and energies. We trade off, and right now he is doing about three quarters of the chores; it just happened."

The married women who manage multiple roles easily have gradually evolved a way of sharing their anxieties, anguish, hopes, ideas, and problems with their husbands. The relationship is a comfort and helps the woman handle the external world with greater ease and security. There do not seem to be any formulas for establishing such a relationship; they are varied and very personalized.

CHILDREN

A woman's children can be both reassuring friends and stress-causing responsibilities. Children's demands on a single parent are great, and this situation will be discussed before parenting shared with a spouse. Divorced women with primary responsibility for their children have to be concerned about the total care and needs of their children, but they express joy in having the children and in the satisfaction they derive from the children's lives. The children may take pride in any accomplishment of the mother and learn how to be participating, contributing members of the family. Many of these children learn how to do housework and chores very early. They learn how to share the ups and downs of the primary adult in their lives, and they learn what family bonds are. Women often acknowledge needing the children to fill what might be a great void in their lives.

Divorced women are forced to assume a more independent role in family decision-making than they might if still married. Some talk about the satisfaction of being able to take care of themselves and their children. Some speak of relocating, learning how to work without any special training or experience, and how proud they feel to have overcome many obstacles. They speak freely of stresses, noting that they were continual, but they usually maintain that the satisfactions outweigh the strains.

Married women also report that children are an important part of their lives, helping to stabilize their existence and to stretch them. Children need the security of order and impose that need on parents. The stretching comes because mothers are forced to assume many new roles and responsibilities in relationships to children.

They find that the family tends to do more than eat and sleep, thus requiring planning for social and intellectual growth. This often introduces all the family members to new events. Some mothers reported that one of the weekend days was designated for family and that meant a trip to the museum, the park, an ethnic neighborhood and new foods, something that they could all participate in and enjoy. Often the other day is spent doing chores and errands, with everyone participating. Time during the day or evening is usually devoted to bringing the children into contact with the parents, particularly the mother. This time may be at meals or before bed, but it is considered precious time since it allows for a recap of the day and for airing any items that weigh heavy on the heart.

Probably the most difficult aspect of parenting for both one- and two-parent families is their relationship with the schools. Contact with teachers and administrators requires extra effort for working parents and may cost them money in time lost from the job. As a consequence, there are often strains between school and parents; children may bear the brunt of the confusion and antagonism. Parental pressure is often exerted on the child to behave, to do schoolwork well, and to stay out of trouble so that the parents will not have to take time off. Parents ought to insist that schools make adjustments for them; many times school administrators have not thought of alternative ways of including parents.

A related source of stress is child care for children of working mothers. There are very few communities concerned about this problem, and child care when it is available is sponsored primarily by churches and other private organizations. Working mothers, particularly those with preschool children, view child-care arrangements as one of the greatest stresses in their lives. Their concern and anxiety over the physical and emotional well-being of their children tend to sap energy and competence. For most of these women, work is not an avocation but a necessity. Many women are exhausted at the beginning of the workday, since they have had to provide breakfast, nudge the family, give encouraging words, oversee dressing, and give transportation to the children.

In spite of the array of problems associated with children, the good parts of motherhood are what women talk about when they tell of their relationship with their children. As one woman said:

> "My kids are steady little rocks. They are a joy. They are terribly funny. I love to look at my children. They make me feel good. I like to take them with me. They enjoy my company. We have moved from being in some sort of constant 'fight authority' relationship to a very warm one. It's a great satisfaction."

OUTSIDE THE FAMILY

WOMEN FRIENDS

Whatever their family situation, women need other meaningful relationships—particularly friendships with women. They may find their women friends through their work or in the neighborhood, or their friends may be from their school days. These relationships are special in that they are informal and vary in intensity, depending on the needs of the friends and the situations with which they are coping. They are not the gossipy, giggly friendships of girlhood but are a continuation of the deeply supportive relationships of young adulthood. It is these friends with whom women review work and concerns about themselves. They use these friends as a sounding board for their anxieties and frustrations. These relationships are particularly important to women who are working in an office or work setting in which there are few other women. Theresa explained:

> "I found that women's groups were so very important to me about five years ago. I just found them reassuring and comfortable and it was just nice to be around women since my whole day was spent in an office with men. Then I started spending less time in organized groups and more time with Polly and Mary. I just

found that I needed to have some friends who helped me relax, just let me be myself. It is like taking off your shoes when you walk in the front door."

Women report that they talk out their feelings with their women friends and it helps them maintain equilibrium. They find understanding and a mutuality of experience, which is sustaining. The complete professionalism and poise demanded on the job or the complete control needed at home can be put aside for the easy camaraderie of a small group of women friends.

One woman explained it this way: "I find that the older I get, the crazier I start to feel, and the greatest source of keeping me sane is other women. I find that I can eliminate stress by being with people with whom I can be myself." Women can consciously help one another handle their complex roles and responsibilities through a variety of methods. They can share their own styles and techniques and they can provide supportive listening.

RELIGIOUS AND OTHER GROUPS

In years past, the church was the primary institution outside the family, and almost everyone had a religious affiliation. Now, families or individuals no longer automatically seek church membership when they relocate in a new neighborhood or new region. Yet Americans have always been joiners even though a strong theme has been that of individualism. Individuals have come together to share experiences, to find respite from work, or to provide for the social good.

Though the churches and religious organizations are still the center of life for millions, many women have found an outlet, not for their spiritual life, but for their intellectual and social concerns in groups concerned with a specific issue, such as children, consumer issues, peace, etc. They take classes of a wide variety and explore topics, learn new skills, and, more important, meet other people, filling a social need. They come together with other like-minded adults for short periods of time. Many women describe these experiences as refreshing and necessary, removing them from the routine of work and the cares of the family and stretching their minds.

Many groups are focused on personal relationships or they deal with self-improvement. This is an important concern for many women who are seeking meaning as they expand the range of their roles. They value the group as a means of helping them understand and cope with some of their real problems with work, children, family. However, these short-term groups do not fulfill the same function as the church did in an earlier time. Many women find friends in classes and self-improvement groups, and it is possible that the need for relationships drew them into these activities initially.

Women still have a need for organizations that will meet their need for relationships with like-minded women outside their family. They especially need this type of affiliation in an increasingly impersonal and increasingly suburbanized society. Greater and greater distances separate people from institutions so that they can no longer walk or drive short distances, perhaps explaining the popularity of television and radio ministries. However, if an essential part of women's being is the need for relationships, their lack can result in alienation and loneliness.

COUNSELORS

Some women have greatly benefited from more formal assistance in working through some of their feelings with professional counselors—therapists, psychiatrists, psychologists, or pastoral counselors. By seeking professional counseling, many women have found that they could sort out the heavy demands placed on them and could adapt to the pace required. An older woman explained:

> "I owe a great deal to my therapist, because for four and a half years I struggled with who I was and who my husband was. He was finally unwilling or unable to accept who I was, and I instead chose to blame

myself for much that happened. I was helped to come to terms with myself, to know that I could be O.K. with above average intelligence and not brilliance, to know that I was not a bad mother, and to accept that my mother was the best mother that she knew how to be. I learned how to love and that I would succeed and fail and that I would be all right."

PEOPLE AT THE PLACE OF WORK

At work a person's success may be aided by the help of an experienced mentor who gives advice and "shows the ropes." Much of the current literature stresses the importance of a mentor, pointing out that women entering the work force are often deprived of a mentor and possible advancement because they have no one to help them understand the organization and the skills required. I think, to the contrary, that almost everyone entering the labor force and a new job has a mentor. However, most women and men do not enter jobs that are going to lead to the top of the organization, so the mentor, or person who initiates the novice into the rules and style of the organization, tells what is necessary to do the job. He or she probably gives clues as to which persons should be avoided and which are helpful, where materials can be obtained, and how the work is done. This is as much as is usually required. Each of us can take on the mentor role with a new woman employee. We can help her adjust to the work routine and can help her handle new relationships. We can listen and help her sort out any new personal problems that arise. We can reach out and include her in our work life and perhaps in our personal life.

If we were to create a network of new and old women employees, we could help alleviate some of the stress caused by the new job. We could also begin to influence the tone of the organization by making it more human and responsive. This is quite important, since women are usually clustered on the lower levels of the organization in subordinate positions. There is a continual tension between the egalitarian norms of our society and the hierarchical nature of most organizations. Women bear the brunt of that hierarchy without understanding how to handle some of the pressure and fatigue.

SOLITARY ACTIVITIES

Even though women naturally center their lives around relationships with other people, it is terribly important that each woman have time to herself, time to spend on her own. This will enable her to find quiet and solace, to refresh her inner self in order to cope with the demands of others.

Time spent alone is another means of relaxing and reducing stress. This does not mean solitude and no activities, but activities that will help provide a sense of perspective. Many women who are handling multiple roles are able to do so because they reserve some part of their lives just for themselves.

There are many ways in which a woman can enjoy her own company; ask an only child and you will get a long list. However, I will talk about four categories or types of solitary activities that women described as they talked about multiple roles. The four categories are physical, creative, cultural, and contemplative.

PHYSICAL ACTIVITY

Since there are many women to whom physical activity is very important and necessary, I will begin with this category. As I noted in the discussion on growing up, there are many women who have always participated in some form of athletic activity and find that their bodies need continual muscular effort. They have switched from team sports to individual sports, and for many years this group of women were in a definite minority. Now physical fitness is the ideal, and a great many people are doing something to stay healthy through exercise. Running is a favorite activity of women who find that they can rid themselves of tension by running several times a week. Some of them have even found themselves exhilarated by becoming competitive long-distance runners.

More and more women are joining health clubs and spas or are exercising at home. The popularity of exercise classes, exercise books and cassettes is due to that group. Those women who exercise in groups or classes are not really alone, but exercising is not a team activity and is usually something that they have chosen to do on their own. There are women who choose to play tennis, racquetball, or even squash because they find tremendous satisfaction in being able to whack a ball. Several women talked to me about the wonderful release for hostility, anger, and frustration which they obtained from playing tennis.

Dancing is a variation of this type of activity and may span the creative and the more physical. One woman talked of the relaxation she found on coming into her apartment at the end of the day and putting on a record and dancing by herself. She worked with people all day and could find release from all the tensions and concerns that had been shared with her during the day. There are other women who find that the aerobic dance routines on cassettes allow them the same release.

Camping, hiking, climbing, and even strolling are other active ways that women can find to be alone. There are women who enjoy a challenge of camping by themselves. One woman told of the joys of taking her cat into the wilderness and being able to cope with the demands of setting up camp and enjoying the challenge of each day, to the bemusement of the very civilized cat who preferred the car to the wilds. A hike or a stroll or uncomplicated climb can also be a way to refresh one's inner being, enabling one to enjoy the beauties of nature without the need to respond to anyone's comments or questions.

Some women find that even a very low level of physical activity helps them handle their lives. There are some women who have a ritual of beauty care—hair, nails, bubble bath, makeup—which pushes them into a level of self-involvement different from their normal pattern. They allow themselves to move through fantasies wonderfully different from their everyday lives. Many of them must negotiate with their families for time to do this.

Not every woman is interested in physical activity, but even those who think they are not should try something that relies on their bodies and makes few demands on their minds and emotions. The change alone could do wonders to relieve tension and provide new insights into ways of coping with other people and responsibilities.

CREATIVE ACTIVITY

Those women who use creative outlets for their stress often are utilizing experiences and knowledge from their girlhood. Many women who learned to play an instrument or do a craft fall back on those skills in adulthood. They play the piano, guitar, or other instrument for their own pleasure, and lose themselves in the music. They have no intention of being part of a musical ensemble, but they need the discipline of the music and the instrument to move beyond their own cares. Now, creative activity ranges from playing an instrument, writing, painting, and the plastic arts to the homely arts of baking. The latter is more of an outlet for more women than is painting. There are many women who shoo their families out of the kitchen and bake. Many women talked of their need to bake bread regularly because they said they could "pummel the heck out of the bread and feel better."

Many women use knitting, quilting, crocheting, sewing, and other needlework as an opportunity to be productive and to work out their tensions. These arts, of course, are traditional female ones and have not usually been seen as stress relievers. They are crafts that can be done in a group or alone, but many women find them a wonderful way to be alone. One could include working puzzles, crossword and picture, in this category, since they are creative and stimulating in a unique way.

CULTURAL ACTIVITY

Other women find that they are uplifted and refreshed if they spend time alone involved in some type of cultural activity. They may choose to go to a play, a movie, a museum exhibit, an art gallery, the zoo or the aquarium, concerts, or stay home listening to music or reading books. They are consuming the artistic efforts of others, but they are allowed to escape and find relief from their mundane pressures. This type of activity may be a regular part of a woman's life or an occasional activity, but it seems to have the same effect. It can break up monotony and provide a sense of stretching. One can learn how others use energy, and it also provides ideas to women seeking continual ideas.

Vacations alone can also be put in this category of cultural, though this could be argued. If a woman chooses to go to a tennis camp, then it is undoubtedly an active outlet; however, many women choose to take a vacation alone to see a particular geographical or cultural area, one that their family or friends do not value. They may choose to visit family in a distant part of the country or go to a resort where there will be others, but the travel will be alone, thus allowing them considerable time to think, view, and assimilate experiences.

CONTEMPLATIVE ACTIVITY

The last broad category is that which I label "contemplative." It is of an entirely different nature and probably appeals to an entirely different type of woman. In other words, it is not an outlet for everyone. This type of activity fills a need for the woman who yearns for solitude, who craves to be away from the noise and distraction of others. Many women find that they need the opportunity for an occasional retreat, organized by a religious sponsor or themselves, to get their bearings on their lives and slow down. Some women find that they enjoy the meditation, whether of Eastern or Western religious origin, and that it provides them with a discipline and order, allowing them to sort out the many demands and pressures. There are others who organize their lives so that through prayer or prayerful contemplation they are helped to find the quiet center of their being. There are many women who are so much a part of the world and its noise that it is essential for them to find a place of solitude in their home and in their head.

Women should rejoice and be pleased that other women have found ways over the years to keep themselves centered and not engulfed by their responsibilities. They are fortunate in that many of the outlets are traditional ones used by women over the centuries. These techniques and methods should be utilized to provide women with respite from the pressures of the modern world, and women are fortunate that these methods are available to them and can be used without effort. Few men have the luxury of so many ways to relieve stress, nor are they allowed to admit that they need to feel relief. Women who do not know how to find outlets should be encouraged to do so in ways that refresh and recharge them, so that they can cope with their many responsibilities.

We should learn how to utilize stress, since it has value. Creative stress can be a means of keeping us from being bored, of pushing us to learn new skills, to probe new frontiers, to adapt to new conditions, and to explore new relationships. We should use stress in a way that keeps us vital and does not overwhelm us with the press of necessity. We should learn to control not only time but the pressures that impinge on our lives. We should capitalize on these aspects of women's nature which are valuable to our society. We should learn to value relationships and the meaning of those relationships. We women need other people and can make the world in which we live a more livable place if we utilize that need and skill. We should rise to a challenge of our lives, embracing those around us.

CHAPTER 5

Black Women's Versatility

BLACK WOMEN'S CULTURAL HERITAGE

Over the centuries, millions of people have voluntarily come to America seeking religious freedom and economic opportunity. The African ancestors of America's black population, however, did not come voluntarily. They were kidnapped and forcibly brought to the United States as slaves. This is an important historical difference between blacks and people of other races.

In West Africa, blacks who were ancestors of black Americans had a peasant society where women were important to the tribal livelihood and to the economy. African women worked on the farms, tending crops and animals, and were the small traders in villages and towns. They were allowed to acquire and control their own money. Women were often the most important link between generations, since children were frequently enrolled in the mother's family rather than in the father's.

In America, black slave women worked in the fields besides doing domestic chores for the slave owner's family and their own families. In addition, they were used as "breeders" to produce additional slaves, and income for the slave owner.

It was during the period of slavery that great separation between the women of the two races originated. Not only were black women encouraged to bear children to enlarge the slave labor force but also at the same time they were used as sexual outlets for males of the dominant group. White women were idealized and seen as apart from sensual needs, while black women were identified with physical passions and the baser aspects of life. Unfortunately, the women of both groups are still enmeshed in old myths which keep them from discovering their sameness and common womanly qualities.

After slavery was abolished at the end of the Civil War, blacks in the South gained freedom of movement and often exercised it. They moved around in the South and to other regions of the country. However, the majority remained in the South and were bound to the land through tenant farming and sharecropping. The women continued to work in the fields and as domestic servants in white households. During the great migrations northward, black women found employment in the lowest levels of industrial manufacturing and in domestic service. In recent years, black women have left domestic service in private homes but perform many of the same tasks in hospitals, clinics, and office buildings. They have entered clerical and sales forces but tend to be clustered at the lowest levels. They are represented at the managerial level in the most minute numbers. Physical work with few rewards is the usual economic activity of adult black women.

Another myth that stands between the women of both races is the myth of the matriarchy. This distorts the true nature of the black family, making it appear peculiar and pitiable. Media attention on black welfare dependency and teenage mothers often helps emphasize this myth. Even though almost half of all black families are headed by a female, the concept of matriarchy is foreign to the black community. True matriarchal societies, communities, or clans exist primarily in preliterate or primitive societies, to use a more frequent term.

In classical anthropology, a matriarchy is a setting in which the actual head of a family is a woman and the genealogical line is traced through the mother's side of the family. The mother's brother assumes great responsibility for the children instead of the children's father. It has been argued that the black adaptation to life in this country has produced a matriarchal family. This, however, has become an easy way to describe black women with dependent children and no husbands. Many eminent scholars have documented the nature of and importance of the traditional two-parent family in Africa and the moral importance of that family as it was transferred to American soil. Strong families have been documented through slave records, letters, court records, and family histories. External circumstances and conditions have caused families headed by females.

Blacks live and grow up in the same society as whites, but they are separated not only by housing and employment patterns but also by attitudes. The black cultural heritage evolved from slavery and poverty and still evokes memories of bondage and low status. However, despite discrimination and subordination, black women have managed to provide continuity for their families and community. They have helped sustain the groups and have learned how to cope in positive ways.

QUALITIES OF BLACK WOMEN

EXPECTATION OF WORKING

Young black girls do not believe in the "Cinderella Syndrome," common among white girls. The Cinderella Syndrome is a belief in a fantasy which contains a few grains of reality. According to this mythic pattern, the poor mistreated young woman is rescued from drudgery, discomfort, and boredom by a handsome young prince. He selects her over her competitors and detractors and takes her away as a princess to a life of parties, comfort, and ease. Cinderella is liberated from housework, child care, or routine by a man who will always provide for her and care for her.

Black girls are raised with the memory of continuing bondage and the ever-present social and economic realities of American life. They know that they will not be rescued by a prince and that they must be prepared to be self-sufficient, earning their own livelihood. They are encouraged to learn skills and develop their capabilities so that they will be able to find good jobs to make a living for themselves and their families. One mother expressed her concern this way:

> "I think we have to help them learn the most that they can learn. We have to promote self-dignity and self-esteem, but we have to help them learn to compete. I want them to have an education that teaches facts and skills, but even an education is not quite enough. It is because a piece of paper, a B.A., doesn't automatically get you a job. I think we have to teach children reality. I don't want to teach them prejudice, but we have to tell them that if they expect to get anything, they had better get it by learning to compete and be prepared."

As black girls grow up and speculate about their future, work is always a part of those speculations. Many are encouraged to dream about combining job and family. They are inspired to think about college: the parties, social clubs, and help in achieving a status higher than their parents'. They are warned to avoid involvements that might force them into an early marriage and make them sacrifice upward mobility for family responsibilities and a lower-paying position. Mothers worry continually about this aspect of their daughters' lives: "I and many of my friends talk about sending our daughters to parochial school because of the control that the sisters have over them. Those children have better behavior, and the sisters are a lot more strict than the public schools around here. However, I think that today's children are a little bit out of control whatever school you send them to."

In black neighborhoods, there are many examples of people who have failed. One sees the wino begging near the liquor store, or knows of a classmate who had to leave high school to have a baby, or sympathizes with a cousin who wanted independence and joined the Army just before high school graduation. Relatives and neighbors who are hardworking and law-abiding are treated with respect, but everyone dotes on the people who are the exceptional successes. Those who succeed against all odds inspire others and offer demonstration that success can be attained if a person is willing to work hard.

Economic realities keep black girls from ever imagining that they will be "stay-at-home ladies." Their mothers, aunts, cousins, and neighbors may be examples of women with stable jobs, good educations, and handsome wardrobes. Working is the norm, and the few women who do not work full time tend to have poor health or so many children that child care is difficult to arrange. Even the most old-fashioned husbands accept working wives, because economic necessity causes greater equity in the husband-wife relationship.

Even those girls who dream of marrying men of high status—doctors, dentists, lawyers, government officials, teachers—plan to have careers that will complement the work done by their husbands. Their visions of the future world are only a little better than the world they know, so the fantasies are under control. However, their parents often tell them that they can be anything they want to be if they work hard. They are told that they should be independent and that failure is of their own doing. Consciousness of race is constant in parental encouragement and in plans for the future. Youngsters are not only held to realities of the present but are encouraged to prepare for a future in which opportunity will be greater.

STRONG INFLUENCE OF MOTHERS

The link that holds these girls to their obligations and directs them to the future is their mother. Like all mothers, black mothers are taken for granted within the family but are enormously praised outside the family walls. In many respects, the responsibilities are heavier for black mothers than they are for mothers in other ethnic groups. As one mother of six children stated: "I have to provide a safe and secure environment for my children to grow up in and to prepare them to take care of themselves in the future. I suppose that is the traditional role of the mother, whether she is human or animal. I guess that it's partly biological and partly social or cultural. I worry about them a lot, because it is not easy to provide a safe environment in the midst of an unsafe community. And it is especially hard to protect black children and teenagers because they seem to be targets of violence and destruction, both physical and mental. Since I have six children, you can see that I do a lot of worrying."

Black mothers have to be concerned about the present as they are continually involved in taking care of immediate activities to keep the family going while pointing toward the future. They talk about the uncertainty of life for blacks and the necessity of teaching their children how to protect themselves. They also try to help their children learn not to be fooled by blacks or whites who would take advantage of them or harm them. They work at helping the children learn to care for themselves while having the emotional security that comes from being a part of the family.

Learning how to be a family member includes learning to work with other family members, being considerate of their needs and interests. Adult relatives can inspire the children to do their best, to learn as much as they can, to succeed in spite of external pressures. Child rearing is not a solitary venture, even if the mother is unmarried.

There are other relatives who are influential in child raising and take some burden off the mother. The goals and aspirations articulated by the mother or by both parents are reinforced by other relatives. They help transmit the values, traditions, and life goals through contact with the children. This is somewhat unusual in American life among other groups.

Grandmothers, grandfathers, aunts, and godparents are often cited as sources of advice, baby-sitting, companionship, and emotional sustenance. This is probably very necessary for women in precarious economic and social positions in the society. Most black women have been raised in close-knit family settings and find family ties important even when they themselves are physically separated from their family of origin. The telephone and mails, along with frequent trips home, provide the continual contact needed to maintain family bonds. A sense of relationship to family permeated the lives and consciousness of the women whom I interviewed. One of them spoke as follows:

> "My mother and I moved away from the rest of the family when I was a little girl. We wrote back and forth and kept up with the family doings in that way. We would go South on the train each summer. Even though we were miles away, I was raised with the spirit of my grandfather ever present. My mother was influenced by his teachings and preachings, and quoted them daily. It was as if he was giving her advice on how to raise me and about how to conduct her life. I think that it helped sustain her."

I hear many stories of a mother or grandmother who courageously managed to keep a family fed, clothed, and sheltered during hard times or widowhood, or tales of a grandfather who coped with poverty without being defeated. These stories serve a motivational and inspirational purpose in a family. Often the stories center around efforts to overcome or outwit segregation and discrimination. This struggle for dignity often provided the impetus for women to fulfill an obligation and transmit a sense of faith, trust, and confidence to their own children.

LESSONS LEARNED IN GIRLHOOD

Part of these feelings are expressed in traditional American terms and a firm belief in some of the basic tenets of the

American ideology. Like other Americans, blacks have the strong conviction that anyone can succeed if he or she works hard and takes care to stay out of trouble. That one has to work for what one gets is an old belief that is tempered by a realistic understanding of irrational and arbitrary racial discrimination. This realism dictates caution and avoidance of potential trouble. Black mothers indoctrinate their children with values and traditions handed down from a generation that faced continual life-threatening encounters with racism. Even though there are laws that provide protection for blacks today, there is still a cautious approach taught to children.

Some of the concepts often instilled in black children are self-esteem, competence and respect for competence, hard work, the need to have marketable skills and an education, an orientation to the future, upright behavior, staying out of trouble, and the ability to find happiness in difficult circumstances and at odd times. The women talk of how important it is that their children develop a sense of self-esteem so that they can cope with prejudice and discrimination. Then they will have survival mechanisms to help them avoid emotional and physical destruction. The children are barraged with maxims, examples, and encouragement designed to make them aware of themselves and their potential. This potential, however, can only be realized if the child fulfills the expectations of the parent. Working hard and well are considered keys to attaining material well-being and protection within the system. "Staying out of trouble has two faces," according to a mother of three children, "one white and one black. Being black is sometimes a hazard, so I tell my children to apply themselves to their work and what they can really do. Sometimes it seems to me that they are acting like somebody is brainwashing them into believing that they can't do the job. I feel that I have to keep encouraging them to do a better job and be more interested in education."

Black mothers then help their children learn how to balance parental aspirations and pitfalls of society. The children are extremely fortunate if their parents have had the education and experience that enable them to interpret the society. One woman expressed it this way:

> "Black children have to be prepared on two levels. They have to be themselves and at the same time prepare themselves until we, as a people, can provide the wherewithal needed. They must get preparation from this society the way it is now, and they must learn what is important to know. We have to be really firm with our kids, because as I remember my own mother saying, 'I'd rather kill you than have the police do it.' This kind of protection black parents have had to give their children, overprotection and training in obedience of a type that white parents don't know about."

The concerns of many black women were summarized by one woman in this way: "I have a feeling of appreciation when I think back on what my mother used to do, and I think that the difference now is that we demand so much of ourselves. We feel responsible to do all the things our mother did. There are things we feel that we should do for our children, to give them opportunity to come around. There is a sense of continuity and a vision of the future that helps center their lives."

Managing Well with Little

This connection with the past helps black women cope with the pressures of low income and high cost of living. Since most of them have grown up in families with similar financial problems, they have learned from childhood how to live frugally but comfortably. This ability is a special advantage for those women who are divorced and responsible for their children; many white women in the same situation are not as prepared to cope with a lowered income and social status.

Living on little can be a trial, but less so if it is a familiar pattern, as it is for most black families. The diet of Southern or Caribbean families utilizes the most economical cuts of meat and vegetables, high in protein and low in cost. Thus soul food nourishes bodies and cultural memories without tremendous expense.

Housing, though, is a problem because it tends to be expensive. Blacks, like most Americans, wish strongly for safe neighborhoods, although many low-income neighborhoods are a constant source of anxiety. Concern for safety has increased the number of blacks moving to suburban areas. Even though many blacks have lived in modest or substandard housing, they have always wanted to brighten up the home and make it attractive. Pictures of Jesus and angels have been favorites, along with pictures of flowers, political leaders, and family.

It has long been considered important to have a nice home, to dress stylishly and "put on a good front" while on a modest income. Many of the ideas of home furnishings and clothing styles were probably originally borrowed by black domestic servants from the period of slavery through the late 1950s. Blacks were constantly exposed to the lifestyles and behavior of upper-class affluent whites and were influenced by what they saw, heard, and the castoffs they were given. For a time the quality of the castoffs was used as a measure of the economic status of the white employer, and comparisons were made by members of black groups. This "hand-me-down" wardrobe was put together with imaginative touches to contrast with the drabness of the workaday uniforms of domestic or menial service. Imitating "rich white folks" provided release from the humiliation and frustration of a segregated life. Some of the imitation was done consciously, some in fun, and some in defiance. The result was positive in helping blacks understand the white world better and gave them some perspective on their own lives.

Such imitation also allowed blacks to show to the world that they were not beaten down, but were doing well. This theme dominates the stories, humor, music, and philosophy of black women. It is one of the motivating forces behind their concern with personal and family cleanliness and with "looking good." One of the earliest black millionaires, Madame C. J. Walker, capitalized on this desire and introduced cosmetics and hair preparations for black women. She pioneered the concept that black women should look their very best in order to fight negative stereotypes and bigotry.

Strategies and planning are needed to stretch small incomes, and black women are aware that they have developed this expertise over many generations. They have internalized the old Yankee adage, "Make it, make do, make it over, or do without." They have learned how to sew, design clothing, alter hand-me-downs, watch for bargains, use layaways, and improvise in creative ways.

BLACK WOMEN'S RELATIONSHIPS

Like all women, black women rely on relationships and do not attempt to handle by themselves their many tasks. They particularly rely on the support of their families, their church, and community organizations.

FAMILY

Black women need the comfort of the family even if they are not physically near their family of origin, because a strong sense of connectedness to family provides protection from the prejudice that they face daily.

The bond created during girlhood is very important. An unmarried woman working in New England explained her need for family identification in this way: "I would be very lonely here if I didn't have some people to turn to. I guess that it has been difficult for me, because I am single, and I am expected by the other people in my office to do more since I don't have a family. I have created a family. I cling to my black friends here who do have families. I have become very close to them, because I find that it makes life more bearable."

The members of a family provide embracing, supportive relationships and role models for the children. A married childless woman described her experience:

> "My mother was an ordinary working-class woman. She worked hard and was active in her church, which consumed most of her time. I would watch her and see what was fun or important. But the woman who I admired the most was my aunt; she was not married and had no family obligations in the way that my mother had. She had all of us, of course, but no full-time family obligations. She was glamorous, because she had more money than anyone else in the family and could spend it on things that were exciting. I think she gave me an idea of what I wanted to be. I think I am now fulfilling the same role for my nieces, who watch me with a kind of awe and respect and want to achieve the same type of life."

Family relationships are especially important to divorced women. However, black women's adjustment to divorce is made easier because of two factors: work and community attitudes. Black women, by and large, have been employed before and during their married lives, so they are not suddenly forced to find a job. It is not easy to assume complete responsibility for the economic, physical, and emotional care of children, but these women fall back on the survival skills of other women in their family and on their jobs. They cut back on many of their expenditures and often get some small amounts of money from other relatives. Furthermore, the black community is tolerant of divorce, though not condoning it. Separation of spouses has been a fact of life for a very long period of time. It began with the slave trade, continued through the period of slavery and the great migrations to the North. Economic hardship often caused separation as husbands would drift away looking for better jobs. Consequently, divorce has been prevalent and accepted in black communities for many years.

Children and husbands are also important to the stability of these women, as they are to all women. They share the household responsibilities in a way that is very natural since usually both black spouses work. The children learn early how to do housework and outside chores, take care of siblings, cook, and assume a major share of the work necessary for the well-being of the entire family. Often any outside earnings of the adolescent children are added to that of the parents or are used for the youngsters' clothing and recreational expenses. Cooperation is a major theme of black families, as is also reciprocal admiration, which helps give confidence to deal with a potentially hostile world.

There exists some tension in husbands' expectations, however, as stated by a middle-aged woman who had remarried and was putting together two families:

> "I think a lot of our men wonder why we can't be satisfied with being wife to them and mother to the children. My husband thinks but doesn't say it, but it goes like, Why do you have to need something else? Don't I provide you with enough? I think they would like it if we worked part time. That's all right, but when it's a career, I think there are very few men who in their hearts don't wonder. They are proud, but I think they'd like to feel that the family is really the woman's first priority. I really do think they feel that way, even the best of them. I don't think there's anything wrong in it. That's just the way it is. It's almost as if they think they are not doing what they should do if the woman needs to go out in the world and do something also."

Such tension is one part of a major problem in the black community, relationships between the two sexes. The relative economic independence of black women has also resulted in independence in emotional relationships. This problem is magnified for educated women, who outnumber their male counterparts. They often choose not to marry or they marry men with lower levels of education and occupational status. The tensions of economic uncertainty are played out in male-female relationships in ways that are not always positive and that contribute to a pattern of unstable families.

CHURCH

Next to the family, the church is the most important institution for black people. This has been true as long as blacks have been in America. They brought a strong sense of religion, song, and group worship with them from Africa. They adopted the message of Christianity with a zeal unmatched by other groups of converts because the Old and New Testaments were the living gospel. They could identify with the ancient Hebrews—the exiles and enslavement and the words of the prophets. The example of Jesus provided a hope for a better future in this or in the next world. Even though gatherings of slaves were illegal, there were slave owners or members of their families who felt that the slaves must be good Christians and worship together. The slaves found different meanings in their interpretation of the Bible than did the owners, and the slaves fashioned songs from the stories, songs expressing the anguish, the faith, and the hopes for freedom and for treatment as human beings.

Christianity became the focal point of life for blacks after slavery, as it had been during the slave experience. The church embodied the yearnings, hopes, and aspirations of the oppressed people. The church was the center of the black community, the source of the intellectual and political leadership. Black women have always given their time, labor, and devotion to the care and activities of the church, and in turn, they have received comfort, uplift, and social status from their involvement. The church is the largest institution that is controlled by blacks, and women have provided the stability to sustain the organization through the years since emancipation. They have been involved in the usher boards, the choirs, Sunday schools, and missionary programs. They have raised money to support the work of their local church, church-sponsored schools, and missions in this country and in Africa.

The churches have served as the social center of the black community, providing positive alternatives to the morally undesirable activities available. Black women could go to church every evening and all day on Sunday, and many of them could learn leadership skills in the context of the church. In the workaday world, a woman might be a maid or have a low-status job, but she could be transformed into a respected leader with prestige in her church. The tenure of many ministers is dependent on their relationship with the female members, particularly the opinion leaders. Even if the women work behind the scenes or primarily with those programs for women and children, they provide the backbone of the church and are recognized for that role.

OTHER ORGANIZATIONS

Many women find relationships and community status in secular organizations, which are such an important part of the black community. These groups range from informal social clubs based on friendship groups to the more formal fraternal organizations in which membership is conferred by a vote of the members. The masonic organizations cross social and occupational lines, while the Greek letter organizations are based on college experience and have a more select membership. All of these organizations endow their members with respectability and opportunities for social activities with others like themselves. In this vast network of communal life, women tend to hold leadership positions only if the organization is an all-female one.

Membership in associations not only helps provide black women with another identity beyond the family and the church, it helps reinforce their ideas of respectability and proper behavior. Blacks often feel that it is very important to counteract the stereotypes about blacks being "loose and loud." As a result, great emphasis is placed on propriety, restraining the passions of premature or permissive sexuality so that the baser physical sides of human nature are not given free rein.

These organizations also serve children and give them a sense of belonging to a community larger than the immediate family. Organizations underscore the teachings of the family about morality. Children are offered ample opportunities to meet peers and to participate in wholesome afternoon and weekend activities. The young people learn how to plan and organize parties, pageants, plays, suppers, fashion shows, teas, luncheons, and dinners. They learn to work together on common projects while having a good time. They learn proper social behavior, how to make small talk, how to dress appropriately and attractively, and how to be a part of an active social group. Religious teachings are often tied into the fabric of the organizations in the rituals and values, and the message reinforces that of the family while helping to blunt the edge of discrimination.

Black parents encourage their children to belong to groups, to be exposed to other adults with similar values and expectations, and to have a cushion of caring created by bonds of color. The children learn what type of behavior is demanded, how to be restrained, and that their behavior reflects on the family.

Girls are involved in many activities, sports, and lessons, all directed toward learning new skills. Most important, however, is that girls are directed toward the major ingredient in life: work.

In spite of the pressures of being at the lower end of the economic and occupational ladder, of having fewer alternatives available, black women manage to maintain optimism and perspective about their lives. There is a continual tension between their hopes and the realization that those hopes may not be fulfilled. Helen, the mother of four children and a social service worker put it into the following words:

"I think minority women are far more pressured than white women. When we go to school, it's job-related. We don't go to school for education's sake. It is fine to pursue some esoteric topic, but the reality is that you go to school to get credentials to get a job to make a living. In that process, you sort of create a mind-set that you are going to be successful at this thing, whatever it is. Being successful means being efficient, articulate, and even acquiescing to a number of things. Our families and our community suggest that there are certain ways to look, walk, and act, and that there is a myth of the strong black woman. Like a lot of myths, it is a myth, but there is a certain amount of strength that we have to carry on. If you carry on over a period of time, it is something you go on doing. It becomes a natural state until that state itself becomes all there is."

WAYS OF COPING

"Carrying on" does become a way of life, but it has its price. Black women, like their white counterparts, experience stress. They talk of headaches, fatigue, short tempers, backaches, stomachaches. Unlike many of the complaints of white women, which seem to be caused by difficulties coping with or integrating roles, black women find that external sources are most often the cause of their pain. They cite instances and examples of prejudicial behavior as the most frequent source of stress. In a way they are able to cope with prejudice and discrimination because they have been trained from childhood to handle them. Even though blacks cannot change society, they can control their own reactions and, perhaps, change the people operating in the immediate environment. Black women, then, are better prepared to handle discrimination against women in the workplace than white women who are unprepared for any prejudice.

DETACHMENT

Black women know that work is a necessity, but are aware that work and employment may be less permanent than other aspects of their lives. Since the labor market fluctuates and blacks are most often the "last hired and first fired," there is an acceptance that job success may be temporary. This is even true of women with professional training and jobs in the public sector. As a result, black women tend to have less of an emotional investment in an organization or a particular job since they might be cut out of that relationship at any time. Perhaps their mental health is protected by this ability to be somewhat remote and objective about their work situations. This is one of the protective strategies they use to cope with discrimination.

SEPARATION OF WORK AND SOCIAL LIFE

A sense of detachment is a way that black women have of separating work life from personal life. In some respects, this is very easy to do, because most work relationships between the races end at the close of the workday with each race going off to separate neighborhoods and styles of life. Betty Wallace spoke for many black women when she said:

> "I don't ever want my personal life integrated with my professional life. I've found that in working, the two seldom mix. It's a good idea to keep what you do when you go home among you and your friends and not share it with your colleagues. It makes things easier. Working is work, and I don't find any pleasure in being chummy with my co-workers. I realize that they are not my friends. I realize I am there to perform a function, to do a job, and it goes no further."

At the end of the workday, one goes home to family and friends, which are a buffer against the outside world and offer a chance to shift from work concerns to personal concerns. Many black women find that this is one of the best ways they have of maintaining a sense of equilibrium.

There are some black women who feel that it is necessary to have friends who do not work at the same place so they can keep their interests broader and grow in a way that might not be possible if they all shared the same employment setting. Since many blacks work a considerable distance from their home neighborhoods, friends who do work in the same place may be friends only at work.

Even though most black women are employed in integrated work settings, they are usually clustered at the lowest levels of service and the white-collar sector and heavily represented in the public agencies. There are fewer private businesses and industries that have hired sizable numbers of blacks, so that the efforts to implement equal opportunity laws and ideology have been left to governmental agencies. This means that most black women work in offices or areas where each may be the only black or one of a small minority. The attendant stress then is alleviated by having black friends who understand what the situation is and offer suggestions for coping and who can be people with whom it is possible to relax.

Many blacks do not like to socialize with whites because they feel that they must put on a mask and be unnatural. Cathy, a young woman in her late twenties, explained her opinion:

> "I need to have some separation. I would not want to leave my office and continue a discussion of all the stressful situations when I get home. I need to feel that I'm going to be able to relax in some way. Besides, I feel we have to make some kinds of cultural distinctions because black people, particularly black women, socializing with whites is a relatively recent phenomenon. Black people and white people as a rule socialize differently, and when we do integrate the two, the form is not the average black person's primary form of socialization. It is seen as a necessary evil. When black people really want to socialize, they go to other black people."

This then is a continuation of the old custom of relaxing with other blacks who understand and suffer the blatant and subtle aspects of racism, compare incidents, and laugh at their oppressors. They do not have to pretend that they are pleased with the situation and the relationships related to work, and when they are with friends it is possible to vent their feelings. This exchange is important because it provides the women with another outlet, and they do not need to take their anger out on themselves. Humor is a saving grace of blacks and is one of the survival techniques that has helped them endure.

Having friends who are not associated with work also provides a distinct change of pace. The friends can get together or go shopping, engage in leisure sports or recreational activities. Women's energies might be directed toward a social club, church, or other activity with friends. This takes their minds off work and relaxes them in a very significant way. They are forced to think of another sphere of life and thus engage in other interests than work.

LEISURE ACTIVITIES

Black women are very conscious that they must spend time in recreation and being creative in their leisure pursuits. They learned early in their lives that they must not totally immerse themselves in any one task, whether it be work, household care, church, or political activities. They have learned that it is important to maintain a sense of self and well-being and that this can be done by balancing the parts of their lives. Some women choose active sports such as tennis, racquetball, or swimming as means of alleviating stress while keeping fit. As one woman said, she can take out tremendous hostility on a tennis ball and not hurt anyone.

Dancing is very important to blacks and is one of the cultural activities that distinguishes them from many whites. It is an activity that is not considered to be for young people only, but for all ages. It is a healthy heterosexual activity that provides the dancers with exercise and often provides an outlet for creative energy. So, black house parties and organizational affairs almost always feature dancing as a very big part of the evening. Blacks are often critical of white social events because there is no dancing, and whites "just stand around and talk."

Singing is another popular leisure activity and is most often carried out in the context of the church. Most black churches have several choirs, and gospel groups are prevalent in black neighborhoods. Festivals and competitions on local, regional, and national levels often are the focus of the choral groups' activities so that in addition to rehearsing they must raise money for costumes and travel. Then there are young people who sing popular songs and work on routines which they hope will propel them to fame. Music always has been an outlet and will continue to be an important one.

Another very important recreational activity is connected with "looking good." Black women have always found it very important to dress well and attractively. They use this means of asserting themselves as women and of maintaining a sense of self-worth. They spend time shopping, finding bargains so that they can stay within their income levels while looking expensive. They also spend a larger portion of their income on hair care and cosmetics than white women do. They find ways of using this as stress-reducing factors. Josie, a middle-aged office worker, told me: "When I get home, I go into my bedroom and carefully comb my hair. I make up my face and try to look as pretty as possible. Then I put on my apron and go into the kitchen to start dinner. It may sound silly but it helps me to relax and move from being my work self to my real self." Other women reported that they devoted some time every week to beauty care, taking long bubble baths, fussing over their wardrobes, and entering into other frivolous but fun activities that provided relaxation and enhanced their sense of well-being.

These activities may seem out of step with the "new woman" as she is described by the media and the more militant leaders of women's groups. Yet they are consistent with black women's historical outlets. Black women are not obsessed with spending time on beauty. These are but small acts that help them maintain sanity in a sometimes insane environment, acts that help them maintain self-esteem in spite of being held in low esteem by the larger society. These self-affirming activities have contributed to the happiness of women over the centuries.

Another way that black women find an outlet for positive energy is in cooking. They too find that baking is a way to relieve tension and stress, and many black women talk of the comfort they derive from cooking soul food. Often, a big cooking spree is an opportunity for a spontaneous gathering of family and friends.

FAMILY HELP

Most black women include the family members in carrying out the domestic chores, as we have seen earlier. All members of the family are expected to share responsibilities for caring for the house, the yard, and chores associated with everyday life. The children are started early so that they learn how to work and the value of work. Since the expectation is that all blacks will have to work to earn a living, they are taught within the family and are not protected from work.

WORK ETHIC

Black women talk of being indoctrinated with the work ethic and having a genuine concern that their children understand and accept that ethic. They work hard even though they have some problems with the lack of acceptance of the ethic on the part of their supervisors and co-workers. They tend to worry about the quality of the work done by their work unit, almost as if poor quality will be blamed on them. They complain of sloppy work done by their work colleagues and supervisors, and as one woman explained: "We are so committed to the work ethic, and it makes me sick to see how the people who established the work ethic behave. They don't do a darn thing if they don't have to, while we're committed to it and drain ourselves." Some of the older women react to this feeling and the ways in which they have brought up their children to do household chores. They express a sense of regret and urge their daughters not to repeat the pattern. One older woman said that she had advised her daughter when she got her first job: "You should build it into your budget to have household help so that your Saturdays will be free. You can take off, go, do what you want, and you don't have the hassle of feeling guilty about your house if someone drops in."

Perhaps the best strategy that black women have for coping with work and their lives is that they accept work as a part of their lives. They work because of necessity as have generations of their female relatives so that the conflicts are less about personal fulfillment than of survival. There is an ingrained sense that work is precious and precarious because of the continual low position of black women on the economic ladder. It is then that these two factors, necessity and impermanence, provide not only the best coping strategies for black women but also separate them from their white sisters.

All women have much in common which the artificial barriers of race prevent them from sharing. Since white women are increasingly in the labor force to stay, they could adapt some of the attitudes and techniques of black women and find their understanding of work and themselves would be enhanced. Blacks' more realistic attitude toward work and its place in life would be helpful to white women who are barraged by many confusing messages. Those messages have little meaning to black women who have no options available. They work with the hope that someday in some small way they will be rewarded. They have faith that the last shall be first. However, they know that the greatest reward is the one they feel in their achievements.

CHAPTER 6

ᏁᎾᎦᏐᏗ

Developing Your Own
Model of "Success"

"Women can't be given high positions of leadership, because they don't know how to make the tough decisions," earnestly says the lanky middle-aged chief executive of a multimillion dollar organization. This statement reflects a stereotyped view of men's experience and of women's. In fact, women have for centuries made tough decisions, but in the sphere of personal relations rather than the world of paid work, which deals often with things and money. Now that many women have paid employment, they are being judged by standards that have been developed by and for men. Are such standards really appropriate? Should women try to conform to men's ways of acting? Are achievement and success the same for all, men and women alike? Women must examine carefully the standards we strive to meet. It is particularly important to evaluate stereotyped views and come to an understanding of our own good qualities as women and as individuals.

MALE MODELS OF SUCCESS

Men's styles of personal life and work have been studied by two researchers whose conclusions are particularly interesting. Michael Maccoby studied men in corporations. In a way, he was attempting to update the 1950s "Organization Man," to see how he functioned in the 1970s. He describes four types of managers, the successful men in American business organizations. One type is the "craftsman," upholder of traditions in all aspects of his life and work. Another is the "jungle fighter," who fights his way through the meanness of the jungle and over others. A third, the "company man," loyal to the organization and concerned for security and calm for himself and for the company. Fourth is the "gamesman," whose primary aim is to win the competition. Men of these four models share a concern for process and for things rather than people. They concentrate their efforts on making the organization go while enhancing their own power. Maccoby emphasizes the newest example of male leadership, the "gamesman," who not only wants to win but knows how to play the game with a team. Nevertheless, this study of organizations and managers shows that there is little concern for people and for the environment in which they work.

An important study of the developmental stages of American adult males was done by Dr. Daniel Levinson, psychologist at the Yale University School of Medicine. He and his staff conducted interviews and constructed biographies of forty men in order to understand more of the nature of men's lives. It is clear from these findings that men tend to be relatively inflexible in their roles or move between roles with relative difficulty. Levinson found that men tend to concentrate on one primary developmental task during the stages of their lives, often giving highest priority to those activities outside the sphere of personal relationships. At all stages men seem to emphasize relationships less than women do, though relationships are perceived as important by the men themselves. Men report fewer adult friendships and less dependence on people than women do.

IS WOMEN'S SUCCESS DIFFERENT?

Some of the current programs to train women to move into traditionally male roles maintain that women must reverse traditional women's qualities and be more like men. In this view, women should be physically strong, less concerned about details, less persistent and stubborn about completing tasks, more competitive, willing to take risks, more career-minded, and more objective in their relationships with others. These demands must be considered, since women will spend most of their lives working. Work for pay is a necessity for today's women and will dominate and satisfy them even if they take time out to raise children.

If women are going to spend most of their lives working, do they want to behave and respond in the same way as men do? Although we do not know if this is possible, the question is valid. Should women attempt to be smaller versions of men or do they have something of value to offer to the workplace and the society which might transform the workplace and the society?

Misleading Images

A slide program used to train women to be managers exemplifies some of the confusion about styles of men and women. The slide tape was put together by a group working for equality and justice for women. The producers of the film use it as a discussion aid in women's groups by examining the lives and careers of three women.

The first woman is an assistant superintendent in a middle-sized school district. The camera follows her daily routine while she describes what is happening. She explains a dizzying routine of meetings, letters, memos, phone calls, and school visits which make up her day and night. She meets with teachers, administrators, parents from morning until late at night. She catches up on mail and

memos in odd moments and impresses us with the variety
of pressures, deadlines, and demands made on her. She has
no personal time or personal life according to the narration.
Unfortunately, she neglected to tell the interviewers and
the producers that she had a husband and two children; this
information might have made her a more real woman to the
audience.

The second woman is black and is the administrator of a
special program for minority children. She starts out with
breakfast meetings and maintains a madcap schedule with
little time for lunch or reflection. She mentions that she and
her husband, whom we do not see, meet every evening for a
bite to eat and a swim at the YMCA. She then goes back to
work for the evening, attending meetings or catching up
with the work on her desk. She often does this six days in
every week.

The third woman is a middle manager in a large public
agency. She is shown in her office, talking on the phone,
working with her staff, attending meetings, and, surprising-
ly, getting her son dressed. Her husband, shown in the
scenes in her home, goes unmentioned although she talks
of her son and their relationship. This woman tells of the
stresses and strains she faces with the enormous amount of
work which she attempts to complete every day.

This slide tape gives a very good picture of many woman
managers and their misdirected energies. They ignored
some of the most important people in their lives and gave
the impression that these people did not matter. They
stressed, instead, the nature of their jobs and the problems
they confronted rather than drawing on some of their
strengths. It was an accurate portrayal of the three particular women, whom I know. Unfortunately, the film conveys
a questionable message to women wanting to assume
managerial positions. It de-emphasizes relationships with
families and exposes the problems which women are creating as they attempt to behave like workaholic men while
being women. They have adopted some of the worst fea-

tures of male managerial behavior. These women are conforming to the dehumanizing nature of the workplace.

WOMEN'S POSITIVE CHARACTERISTICS

Women need to bring to the work environment their characteristics which are distinct and unique, thus beginning to transform the organizations and work settings. We need to use those strengths which are ours rather than attempting to adapt to those less familiar and perhaps alien to our natures. What are those characteristics and how do we define criteria based on them? The women in the film show what not to do: to graft male patterns of behavior onto female responses and patterns. The result is a frantic, frenzied style marked by fatigue, cynicism, and a harsh quality in their lives.

Most observers and researchers concerned with the quality of women's lives and their feminine characteristics agree that women are different from men. Scholars like Carol Gilligan, Carolyn Heilbrun, and Jean Baker Miller hail as a most vital quality of women what has been denigrated if not ignored, the need for and the ability to nurture relationships. Women find meaning in relationship to others, not in separating themselves from people and feelings, as many men do. Women are concerned about helping others to grow and express themselves, helping them to attain satisfaction. Perhaps this nurturing comes from the female biological role. Women define themselves with reference to those persons close to them rather than by the activities in which they are involved. These scholars urge women not to fear entering the fray and assuming the power of dealing with it, but they urge that women enter as women, not as imitation men. Women have the innate ability to create, to care, and to encourage growth, all in the context of concern for others and with others. We should use this ability in ways that will enable each woman to fulfill her own potential and that of others.

What does this message mean to you? Let me show what it means to me by a personal illustration. As a senior staff member of a large public agency, I was enveloped by the maleness of the agency. However, I could naturally assert my ideas and plans in the context of my experience as a woman. In contrast, another senior woman manager attempted to be "one of the boys" by hanging out with them after work and imitating their behavior. She had taken on the "tomboy syndrome" in attempting to be a man and to be accepted as a man by her male peers. Yet because she tried this imitation, the men tended to dismiss her as a serious colleague and thus missed many of her good ideas about agency problem-solving and management. I had better luck, always reminding the men that I had different perspectives, but that we all gained from the diversity. I gained the respect of my male colleagues and in addition, I became a confidante of many of the staff, male and female, clerical and professional. As a result, I acquired greater knowledge of the agency, the problems and nature of the relationships. I, in turn, could use the information in ways that helped the staff function more effectively and move the organization toward fulfilling its goals. This is an example of how womanly qualities can enhance power.

However, we must be careful not to seek power for the sake of power. This can lead to corruption of our ideals and purpose. Power is best shared with others, and then it becomes a transforming force. Power is most meaningful when it can be used to help people and organizations realize their potential. Women have to learn how to use this ability rather than to fear power in the hands of others.

We women should begin to accept and be proud of those characteristics which are feminine, womanly, rather than regret them. We should capitalize on our strengths rather than view those strengths as weaknesses. We certainly know enough about power and the ways in which it is used by those in command of our society, world, and lives. We can see that power is used to inhibit individuals and groups of people rather than develop them and their abilities. If we adopt the authoritarian means, we will not have helped to transform ourselves or our world. Think about the people you know who make the decisions about your business or organization, your city, nation, world. Now examine the ways in which those people gain compliance. Do they use terror, fear, or threats rather than begin a dialogue and enlist those affected by the decisions? Do they tend to use one style consistently rather than search for different methods or encourage diversity? What would you do that would differ in style or content?

ORGANIZING AND PLANNING

Let's talk about the ways in which you can set priorities and develop methods to help you handle multiple roles with ease and flexibility. First, I think you will agree that being able to handle multiple roles is an asset and provides advantages in many spheres of life. As we all learn sooner or later, it is impossible to do everything at once or even as many things as we would like to do. Many women have discovered by trial and error over the years that they have to learn to set priorities so they do not lose control of their lives. How does one do this if it is not a habit? Well, in the long run, it is easier actually to follow a plan rather than to rush off willy-nilly. Since methodical habits are formed by performing rather mechanical steps, so too, in setting priorities, you will need to begin in a mechanical way until you automatically set priorities for the short- and long-term goals in your life.

DEFINING YOUR GOALS

You can start setting priorities by making four charts for four separate periods of time: Six Months, One Year, Five Years, and Ten Years. Take a single sheet of paper for each period of time so that you can conduct the exercise in an expansive way. We don't want to cramp your thoughts or keep you from exploring all the possible ideas which might flow into your mind. Label each paper across the top with one of the four headings, then make vertical columns with the following labels: Goal to Achieve; Realistic; Dream; Skills Needed; How Attain Skills; Methods to Use; Indicators of Attainment.

Now start listing goals. You should not make these charts heavy with intangible goals such as "happiness." You should be specific and define what happiness will mean. It could mean learning a new language and taking a trip to a foreign country where the language would be used. It could mean taking your closet apart, rebuilding it in a more functional manner, and discarding the items that cause disorder within. Your list of goals should reflect your inner needs, as well as your everyday self. Make sure that there is a good balance.

Now fill in the corresponding columns.

Why should there be the labels "Realistic" and "Dream"? This is necessary because in all honesty you will be forced to tell yourself which goals you will be able to accomplish in the time specified. You may have to move some particularly difficult goal to a larger time frame. It is also helpful to distinguish those goals which are fantasy and recognize that they are really a part of yourself. We all need fantasies to provide release from tension and stress, and allow our imagination free rein. Yet we should be able to distinguish the possible from the totally impossible. One of my favorite daydreams, one of many, is to be a television personality. This notion has no connection with my real world since I am not related to the entertainment industry nor am I likely to do anything which would move me into that circle. I am also past the age when television personalities begin their careers, but this factor doesn't matter since the idea is all a fantasy anyway. If I write it on my list, I need to write down that it is a dream. However, not all daydreams are totally unrealistic, and you may find a way to make yours realistic. More power to you if you can.

Next, it is necessary to define the skill or skills needed to attain a particular goal. If you list all the skills needed, you will begin to understand that goals are achieved by hard work. You should break the work into the smallest parts in order to achieve the goals. For example, rebuilding and reorganizing the closet may require the skills of sketching, sorting, cleaning, carpentry, sewing, plastering. You will need to determine if you have the right skills or if you will need to borrow or pay for the skills to achieve the goal. You might decide that certain skills you need but do not have would be helpful to you in the long run. In that case, you could take a course or some courses to gain the knowledge needed. Then you will enter that in the column for how the skills will be attained. If learning the skills is going to take a long time, you should reassess whether the goal is in the right time slot. The process may take you longer than you think, and the schedule may be unrealistic. You should not set yourself up to fail.

Next, when you begin to plot out methods, you might want to list the ways in which you will proceed in a step-by-step manner. This means that you put down the first step at the top of this list and proceed to outline each subsequent step. In this way you will begin to see how complex are your tasks and your goal.

You will begin to develop the proper strategies needed to accomplish the goal. Achievement does not come out of a vacuum but results from planning, strategy, and drudgery. Let's return to the example of rebuilding the closet to see how this is implemented. You might first decide what will have to go into the closet. You might develop an inventory list of contents. Then you might decide what type of space is needed for each type of item. A sketch of storage devices and use of the space might be the next task. You would plan any structural changes that would have to be contracted for or undertaken by you. Decide what work will take place in what order, including knocking out walls, plastering, carpentry, painting, cleaning, and replacing the items.

The last column, Indicators of Attainment, is another way of stretching your mind to anticipate signs of progress along the way. You should refer to the Methods column since your indicators of attainment might be a mirror image of the

methods. Thus when you have written out an inventory of
the contents of your closet, you will have moved toward
attaining your goal. Each subsequent task will be reflected
on the Indicators side. It may seem superfluous to include
this column, but this is another way to discipline yourself to
think of concrete ways to accomplish your goals.

While planning for six months or a year will be easier
than for five or ten years, you should begin to think of the
distant future in order to begin making it happen. In this
way, you will begin to sort out what is important to you and
to determine how you want to lead your life. You will be
able to plan in a way that makes sense to you. You will
begin to set priorities, place the important and not so
important tasks and responsibilities in the context of your
goals for your life. You will find that this type of life
planning will allow you freedom to distinguish the more
meaningful parts of your life and you will not be tied up in
knots with the less consequential parts.

The more you begin to set priorities and then make them
a habit, the easier the planning will become. Many women
find that they set priorities without even thinking about the
process. Women in their forties and over are the ones most
experienced in this aspect of their lives. They have often
learned not to worry over every event, demand, or request
made of them. They have usually learned to assess what are
the most important items to be taken care of first and what
things don't even need to be tackled. You can learn to make
your roles more manageable by doing the same.

You should not think that by organizing your life according to goals and charts you will become a robot or automa-
ton. Never fear, some of the most feminine women manage
to retain their womanly qualities while being well prepared
for the turns and twists. Organizing one's life does not mean
that spontaneity and whimsy will be banished or that you
will be all hard edges, bruising everyone who brushes
against you. On the contrary, you will be maximizing a
womanly skill in a way that will allow you greater freedom
to be a woman.

NURTURE AND GROWTH

We should not give up our abilities to encompass many responsibilities and roles in favor of the more constricted roles of men. We should attempt to teach men how they can develop their lives and open them to richer relationships with others or activities that will move them beyond work.

A SENSE OF SELF

Women should see the opportunities to be involved with other people as an advantage. However, we should not be consumed by those relationships and subservient to those people with whom we have relationships. We can avoid this centuries-old pattern by developing a sense of self, by assuring that we make clear our own goals and qualities so others will be aware of that self. Women fear that if they are going to have a clear identity, it will mean they are selfish rather than selfless. Selfishness is a condition in which one's total attention and intellect are focused on the self, swallowing up everything and shaping people, events, and activities to accommodate to that one consuming interest. In contrast, a sense of self and self-identity means that the person approaches all others with an openness seeking to respond in a way that respects the personhood of the other. A sense of self allows for growth and communicates pride in what one is and can do. There should be balance so that the woman with this sense of self will be able to be involved without giving up everything she wants: her goals, priorities, values.

The sense of knowing who you are will come from taking time to explore, delving into your innermost being, and sometimes experiencing pain. Those women who maintain that they must have quiet to gain a sense of perspective are doing just that. They find through prayer, meditation, contemplation, communing with nature, that they are able to refresh themselves, to listen to self under the surface. In this way, they begin to understand their own nature and can bring to relationships the maturity and wisdom that gives as well as takes. They learn to listen to themselves and in turn learn how to listen to others. They learn how to sort out the real messages that others communicate.

HELPING OTHERS

Those women who have developed their own sense of self are often generous in helping others to grow. Just as power is greatest and most significant when it is shared, so growth becomes powerful when it is assisted in a nonrestrictive way, not forced but guided. Women who have learned how to handle multiple roles find that they themselves grow when they help others explore their potential or try new attitudes and skills. Those women who help explore and guide rather than push or "do for" are the women who have a sense of adventure and excitement in learning new things.

You will find, as other women have, that satisfaction can come from allowing others to grow, to develop their capacities, and to complete their goals. The greatest satisfaction will come if you can step back so that the person learns to need less future help. You can do this in any setting, at home, with friends, at work, or in your community.

Your growth will be enhanced if you are a part of the adventure of defining problems with others and working toward solutions. The search for solutions will be a way to keep your mind active and alert and attuned to new ideas. Women who are bored are usually not occupied with exploring the new but with continually reworking the old.

Now some women worry that they will fall into a stereotype of women if they are concerned with nurturing the growth and development of others. They fear the nurturing because it marks them as a woman. Yet our society needs a great deal of nurturing to avoid becoming more dehumanized and less humane. We should worry that there is not enough nurturing to avoid alienation. We should try to find ways in which we can encourage nurturers, build them into our human networks and institutions. Women who are comfortable nurturing should do so, because they will change the quality of life in our society. Nurturing is not synonymous with smothering, which concerns some women. They fear that they will be accused of covering up the creative sparks of another person if they offer comfort, support, and affection. Smothering is an aspect of selfishness and occurs when a woman with too little to do concentrates all her energy on one other person.

If you are not a nurturer by nature, and not all women are comfortable in that role, do not worry about it. You should make an effort, however, to reach out to people since we all benefit from relationships with others. If women once again accept nurturing as a natural and a necessary part of life and human nature, and a needed ingredient in our society, then men will be encouraged to adapt some of their styles to meet the need for nurturing. Many men might also begin to feel comfortable with their own instincts to nurture, and repress competitive and aggressive instincts. All of us, both sexes, will gain from this change, but women will have to lead the way.

CONCERN FOR THE ENVIRONMENT

Women tend to be concerned with their context, the environment in which they live and work. This is a feminine quality which should be appreciated and utilized for its potentially transforming power. Again, some women worry that they will fall into stereotypes of housekeeping when fussing about buildings and decoration if they allow themselves to act on this traditional feminine characteristic. However, this type of sensitivity led the early women reformers to crusade to improve city neighborhoods and services so children and families could lead decent lives in clean, healthful surroundings. The concern for the environment was coupled with a faith and a religious belief in life and in service to a higher order. This valuable concern has the potential for changing the world in which we live.

WORK IN CONTEXT

Work, like relationships, should be placed in perspective and not allowed to dominate your life. This can be done by placing work in the context of the larger world and by drawing on ethical moral values. In this way, you will begin to have control over another part of your life. If you allow work to dominate all your waking hours, you will find that your world will shrink, your relationships will diminish, and you will feel as if you are on a treadmill. On the other hand, if you see work as one part of your life, though time-consuming, you will be able to balance the parts of your life and be healthier. If you find that you are being drawn into that small vortex, you can redeem your sense of perspective by turning to the great ethical works of the ages: the Bible, the philosophers of the ancients, the modern philosophers. By allowing yourself the objective view of the eternal questions of good and evil, the nature and destiny of humankind, the purpose of our lives, you will begin to notice that the importance of your job will pale.

In this sphere one can adapt some of the methods and approaches used by black women. They have an easier time placing work in perspective, because of external circumstances and their knowledge that nothing, particularly employment, is permanent. When this fact is fully understood, it means that work cannot be the central force in one's life. There are important areas in which one can make an emotional investment: family, church, community. So, we all need to understand the ephemeral nature of jobs and in our vulnerability avoid making a total investment in work to the exclusion of other parts of our lives.

EVALUATING YOUR ACTIVITIES

You can begin to explore the meaning of various parts of your life by doing another exercise which will begin to be habitual and will help provide you with a sense of balance. On a blank sheet of paper, put the heading "Most Treasured Activities" at the top. Then make four columns, one labeled "Activity," the second "Nature of Satisfaction," and the third "Probable Length of Time"; the fourth column will contain a number. This exercise will consist of making an inventory of all the activities that engage your time and energy. You should list them in column one; just keep writing them down until you have exhausted all the things that you do. You may need several pages with columns. Then go back and carefully think through what you enjoy about the particular activity. For example, you might enjoy the salary you get for your work. Put it down. If you cannot think of any particular satisfaction associated with an activity, leave that space blank. The third column is for you to estimate the amount of time that you are involved in this particular activity within a given month. When you have filled in columns two and three in relation to column one, go back and rank all your activities in importance to you. Put this number in column four. Then take this sheet and compare with the other chart we described earlier dealing with goals how you spend your time. Compare the ways in which the activities do or do not mesh with the goals. You may have to do some reassessment of your time or priorities if there are big discrepancies. When you finish, you might list on a separate sheet of paper the activities that you are not engaged in but wish you were. This sheet might tell you how to shift some gears and spend your time in other ways, particularly in order to accomplish your goals.

When you analyze the Activities chart, you will discover how you are spending your time and how you might change. You might want to spend more time in other activities and find ways to accomplish the same tasks in less time. You might want to refer to some of the time-saving ideas listed in Chapter 3. Each of us must place every part of our lives in perspective, and that perspective should change as our lives change. We may stress work over family at one point in our lives and reverse the relationship at another stage. We may place social relationships ahead of other activities at one time and place them last at another time in our lives. It is important that we understand our activities and how they relate to our life goals. And we should understand motivations: Why we do certain things and what satisfactions are derived from the activity. We should be prepared to discontinue some activities and replace them with others; in this way, we continue to have control over our lives.

DETERMINING YOUR PERSONAL STYLE

These suggestions are really designed to help you figure out how you can best define your individual style. You should not attempt to fit yourself into a mold that someone else has created for you. Most often someone else's pattern will be uncomfortable and will cause problems because it doesn't fit. You should work out the options that are available to you and that enhance your growth and the fulfillment of your goals. You should use your multiple roles to bring you pleasure. Although you will derive pleasure from your many roles, you should recognize that there will be stress. Yet stress itself can be used creatively rather than in a negative fashion.

You should begin to assess those roles which you play and analyze them in terms of pluses and minuses. What do they add to the goals that you have projected? How do they detract from the goals? Are there roles that you should add to your repertoire in order to attain your goals? You should explore who you are through the roles you play. You might try different roles to determine their suitability for you: Do they fit you? What roles would be inappropriate for the life you are leading? You should begin to understand the way in which you are handling your life through the roles you fill as you carry out your multiple responsibilities.

How do you use the energies you possess? How do you put stress to use? Women who are handling multiple roles well express a need for adventure, new experience, and creative use of their energy. Do you like to do new things continually or are you satisfied with a comfortable routine?

If you begin to know yourself better, you can utilize those roles to accomplish your goals and work to realize your potential.

You should determine how your many roles, whether daughter, lover, mother, worker, leader, advocate, mediator, homemaker, risk taker, intellectual, can be integrated into your life. You might want to reassess the role of family, religion, and leisure as you balance the roles you play and strive to put them in perfect order. The order may be perfect today but may be "out of sync" tomorrow. That is in the nature of life. A temporary lack of balance will not be totally disorienting if you know yourself and the ways in which other women have handled their roles.

Taking pencil and paper and going through the mechanical steps outlined above will be a beginning in defining what you do with your life and how you can handle the many demands made on you. There are millions of women leading ordinary lives who manage to juggle many, many roles and responsibilities. They have found ways to understand their lives and handle stress, the outlets needed to keep them sane. They continually probe the depths of despair and the heights of joy, often with the assistance of religious faith. They are learning to live their lives to the fullest extent and are continually expanding their potential. You can do the same.

In some ways, I have spent most of this book describing how women manage their lives by handling the small things in their lives. It is these small things which glue their lives together and allow them to function in many settings and with many roles. You, too, can manage your own multiple roles by adapting methods and techniques, taking pleasure in the small aspects of daily life. You will achieve a sense of satisfaction when you use your energies in creative ways and follow the path of generations of women who have quietly accomplished miracles affecting the lives of people.

Your own model of success will be based on a realistic analysis of your self and your environment, and will be an adaptation of the methods and techniques used by women who successfully manage their lives. The key to handling multiple roles is yourself and your willingness to experiment with the roles and the reality of your life. Women have a great many strategies that enable them to handle multiple roles, and you are a part of the tradition. The result will be your acceptance of the potential you have to be a "super you."

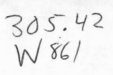